D0362250

The
15
Descriptions
of Love

Other books by Alexander Strauch include:

Biblical Eldership:
An Urgent Call to Restore Biblical Church Leadership

The Study Guide to Biblical Eldership:
Twelve Lessons for Mentoring Men for Eldership

The Hospitality Commands

Agape Leadership:
Lessons in Spiritual Leadership from the Life of R. C. Chapman
coauthored with Robert L. Peterson

Men and Women: Equal Yet Different

Meetings That Work

A Christian Leader's Guide to Leading with Love

Love or Die: Christ's Wake-up Call to the Church

If You Bite & Devour One Another:
Biblical Principles for Handling Conflict

Paul's Vision for the Deacons:
Assisting the Elders with the Care of God's Church

THE 15 Descriptions of LOVE

Applied to All Christian Leaders & Teachers

1 Corinthians 13

Lewis & Roth Publishers

The 15 Descriptions of Love:
Applied to All Christian Leaders & Teachers

ISBN-10: 0-936083-46-8
ISBN-13: 978-0-936083-46-9

Copyright © 2018 by Alexander Strauch. All rights reserved.

Cover design: Bryana Mansfield

**Unless otherwise indicated, Scripture quotations are from The ESV® Bible
(The Holy Bible, English Standard Version®), copyright © 2001 by Crossway,
a publishing ministry of Good News Publishers. Used by permission. All
rights reserved. ESV® Text Edition: 2016.**

Printed in the United States of America
Second Printing 2019

Library of Congress Control Number: 2018966098

To receive a free catalog of books published by Lewis and Roth Publishers, please call toll free
800-477-3239 or visit our website, *www.lewisandroth.com.*

Lewis and Roth Publishers
P. O. Box 469
Littleton, Colorado 80160

Contents

Connecting Love and Leadership

Set the believers an example. . . in love.
1 Timothy 4:12

Much good material has been written describing the leadership qualities of courage, resourcefulness, charisma, conviction, perseverance, visionary thinking, self-discipline and decisiveness. Yet few books on church leadership include anything about love. This is a tragic oversight since *the New Testament is perfectly clear that love is indispensable to the gifts of leading and teaching.*

Indeed, the New Testament mandates that spiritual gifts be exercised in love. As Paul puts it, any attempt at leading and teaching apart from love is like "a noisy gong or a clanging cymbal" (1 Cor. 13:1). To have all of the above leadership qualities but not love spells failure for a Christian leader (1 Cor. 13:1–3).

Furthermore, leaders and teachers set the spiritual tone for the church. They have the power to create a more loving atmosphere within the local church. If they are lovers of God and lovers of people, their followers will more likely be lovers of God and people. If, however, leaders are self-centered, critical, proud, angry, and impersonal, the people will adopt these same ugly dispositions.

Also, in the church family people must work closely together as brothers and sisters in Christ in making decisions and accomplishing tasks. At times this is difficult. Much work within the local church (and among local churches) is done in group settings: elders' and deacons' meetings, staff meetings, board meetings, committee meetings, and all-church meetings.

The longer we work together, the more we get to know one another's faults and annoying personality traits, which can make life together frustrating. Understanding the New Testament principles of love will significantly enhance healthy group leadership, group meetings, and congregational life as a whole. Without love, it is impossible to live and work together in Christian harmony.

I believe that understanding what the Bible says about love would significantly improve the relational skills of our church leaders and teachers and greatly enhance their effectiveness in ministry. It would diminish senseless conflict and division, promote evangelism, and produce spiritually healthy churches. Most important, it would please the Lord.

This book, therefore, is written to leaders and teachers at every level of leadership within the local church. If you lead or teach people—as a Sunday school teacher, youth worker, women's or men's ministry leader, Bible study leader, administrator, music director, elder, deacon, pastor, evangelist, or missionary—love is indispensable to you and your ministry.

As Michael Green so beautifully reminds us, "Love is the most attractive quality in the world. And it lies at the heart of Christianity."* For that reason, God requires that you and I lead and teach with Christlike love and continually grow in our love for him and for all people.

This booklet is an excerpt from the book
A Christian Leader's Guide to Leading With Love.
This shorter version was produced in order to make the material on 1 Corinthians 13:1–7 more accessible to people who do not wish to read the full book.

A study guide is available online at Lewisandroth.com.

---

*Michael Green, *Evangelism Through the Local Church* (Nashville, TN: Thomas Nelson, 1992), 97.

Chapter 1

Five Minus One Equals Zero

I will show you a still more excellent way.
1 Corinthians 12:31

Dwight L. Moody, the Billy Graham of the 19th century, tells of his life-changing encounter with the doctrine of love. It began when Henry Moorhouse, a twenty-seven-year-old British evangelist, preached at Moody's church for a week. To everyone's surprise, Moorhouse preached seven sermons in a row on John 3:16. To prove that "God so loved the world" he preached on the love of God from Genesis to Revelation. Moody's son records his father's description of the impact of Moorhouse's preaching:

> For six nights he had preached on this one text. The seventh night came, and he went into the pulpit. Every eye was upon him. He said, "Beloved friends, I have been hunting all day for a new text, but I cannot find anything so good as the old one; so we will go back to the third chapter of John and the sixteenth verse," and he preached the seventh sermon from those wonderful words, "God so loved the world." I remember the end of that sermon: "My friends," he said, "for a whole week I have been trying to tell you how much God loves you, but I cannot do it with this poor stammering tongue. If I could borrow Jacob's ladder and climb up into heaven and ask Gabriel, who stands in the presence of the Almighty, to tell me how much love the Father has for the world, all he could say would be: 'God so loved the world, that He gave His only begotten Son, that whosoever believeth in Him should not perish, but have everlasting life.'"[1]

9

Unable to hold back the tears as Moorhouse preached on the love of God in sending his only Son to die for sinners, Moody confessed:

> I never knew up to that time that God loved us so much. This heart of mine began to thaw out; I could not keep back the tears. It was like news from a far country: I just drank it in. So did the crowded congregation. I tell you there is one thing that draws above everything else in the world, and that is love.[2]

As a result of Moorhouse's influence, Moody began to study the doctrine of love. This changed his life and his preaching. He later said:

> I took up that word "Love," and I do not know how many weeks I spent in studying the passages in which it occurs, till at last I could not help loving people! I had been feeding on Love so long that I was anxious to do everybody good I came in contact with.
>
> I got full of it. It ran out my fingers. You take up the subject of love in the Bible! You will get so full of it that all you have got to do is to open your lips, and a flood of the Love of God flows out upon the meeting. There is no use trying to do church work without love. A doctor, a lawyer, may do good work without love, but God's work cannot be done without love.[3]

D. L. Moody could not have been more biblically correct when he said, "God's work cannot be done without love." That is the message of the most famous love chapter in the Bible, 1 Corinthians 13.

The More Excellent Way

It is universally agreed that Paul is the greatest pioneer missionary, scholar, teacher, evangelist, and hero of the faith. Yet he knew that all his brilliance, multi-giftedness, and sacrificial dedication meant nothing if it were not bathed fully in love. *No other New Testament writer spoke more about love or provided more practical leadership examples of love than Paul. Through the lifetime ministry and letters of Paul, God gave his church, and all its leaders and teachers, a model of loving leadership.* In all of Scripture nowhere is it more clearly and forcefully stated that love is indispensable to leading and teaching than in 1 Corinthians 13.

Paul wrote this passage in response to disruptions that arose in the church of Corinth regarding spiritual gifts. To correct the church's misguided views of spiritual gifts and its overall self-destructive way of behaving, Paul promised to show the Corinthians a "more excellent way" to live (1 Cor. 12:31). He wanted them to know there is something far more important than supernatural gifts, something that transcends the most excellent gifts and performances, something that if absent will render all gifts worthless. That something is love.

The love Paul speaks of is primarily love for fellow believers. This love was defined by Jesus Christ when he gave a new commandment to all his disciples to love one another "just as" he had loved them (John 13:34–35). This love gives itself in total self-sacrifice for the good of others. Jesus exemplified this new pattern of love by humbly washing the disciples' feet (John 13:4–17) and selflessly sacrificing his life on the cross for others. John puts it this way, "By this we know love, that he laid down his life for us, and we ought to lay down our lives for the brothers [and sisters]" (1 John 3:16).

> "There is no use trying to do church work without love. A doctor, a lawyer, may do good work without love, but God's work cannot be done without love."
> —D. L. Moody

To silence any doubt that love is the "more excellent way" and to jolt the Corinthians' wrong thinking about spiritual gifts, Paul uses all his rhetorical skills to communicate with eloquence and force that love is the "more excellent way." He writes:

> And I will show you a still more excellent way. If I speak in the tongues of men and of angels, but have not love, I am a noisy gong or a clanging cymbal. And if I have prophetic powers, and understand all mysteries and all knowledge, and if I have all faith, so as to remove mountains, but have not love, I am nothing. If I give away all I have, and if I deliver up my body to be burned, but have not love, I gain nothing. (1 Cor. 12:31–13:3)

Let's take a close look at this passage to gain a clearer understanding of what it says.

Without Love
Even Heavenly Language Sounds Annoying

The purpose of spiritual gifts was to build up and unite the body. Yet the Corinthians' enthusiasm over the supernatural gift of tongues caused pride and disorder in the church body. The independent-minded Corinthians used their gifts for personal ego gratification, which caused division within the body.

To correct this distortion, Paul captures their attention by hypothetically picturing himself as "the world's most gifted tongues-speaker,"[4] being able to speak eloquently in "the tongues of men and of angels." Such a gift would have greatly impressed the Corinthians. But Paul declares that even if he had such an exalted experience because of heavenly giftedness, he would be "a noisy gong or a clanging cymbal"—that is, an annoying, loud, empty noise—if he did not act in love, as described in verses 4 through 7. The beauty of his miraculous speech would be distorted without the grace of love.

Paul isn't merely saying that his speech would be a clamorous noise, but that he himself would be a hollow, annoying sound. He would not be what he should be; he would be seriously deficient in his Christian life and not living according to the "more excellent way." The reason Paul would be an empty noise is that he would be a loveless tongue-speaker. He would be using the gift of tongues to glorify and serve himself rather than to serve or build up the church, which is the goal of love (1 Cor. 8:1).

When I teach on this passage, I often use a visual illustration. I pull out from behind the pulpit a steel pot and a hammer and begin to beat on the pot as I talk about spiritual gifts and the need for love. At first, people laugh. They think it is a marvelous illustration. But I keep it up. While I am banging on the pot, I keep talking about spiritual gifts. Soon people aren't laughing or smiling anymore. They have had enough; they're annoyed and getting more agitated by the moment, but I keep banging. When it seems they can't stand it any longer, I stop and ask, "Are you annoyed? Are you enjoying this? Does it please you? Do you find it edifying? Would you like me to continue beating the pot for the remainder of the message?"

Knowledge without love inflates the ego and deceives the mind.

No one wants me to continue beating the pot. At this point I remind them that this is what they are like to others and to God when they use their gifts apart from love. They are nothing more than "a noisy gong or a clanging cymbal."

Without Love
Knowing It All Helps No One

Paul next speaks of himself hypothetically as possessing the gift of prophecy in such full measure that he would know "all" mysteries and "all" knowledge. He would thus have the theological answers to all the mysteries of God that people crave to understand. He would be a walking, talking encyclopedia of knowledge.

Some people love to display their intellect and theological superiority. They are proud of their learning and speaking ability. Such pride had become a serious problem at Corinth. Some people were arrogant because of their knowledge and puffed up with self-importance. They wanted recognition for their prophetic insights and superior wisdom, and they looked down on others with lesser knowledge and giftedness. As a result of their arrogant misuse of knowledge, they harmed the church body (1 Cor. 8).

Knowledge without love inflates the ego and deceives the mind. It can lead to intellectual snobbery, an attitude of mockery and making fun of others' views, a spirit of contempt for those with lesser knowledge, and a demeaning way of dealing with people who disagree. I know of a pastor who had a phenomenal knowledge of the Bible but who hurt many people with his doctrinal scrutiny and divided his own congregation repeatedly until there was no one left but himself. He had a big head but a little heart. His theology was as clear as ice and twice as cold. Such is the path of one who has knowledge without love.

So Paul states that even if he had all-encompassing knowledge, apart from love he would be "nothing"—a spiritual zero. He insists that a loveless prophet, a loveless scholar, or a loveless teacher is worthless to the discipling of God's people. History confirms this, as John Short observes:

Loveless faith and loveless prophecy account for some of the more tragic pages in the Christian story through the ages. It has burned so-called heretics; it has stultified the sincere quest for truth; it has often been contentious and embittered; and it has often issued in the denial of Christian brotherhood to fellow believers.[5]

In a similar vein, George Sweeting, former president of Moody Bible Institute, makes this observation: "I have been keenly disappointed to find people more concerned about hidden mysteries than about needy people.... Too often Christians are concerned about hidden truth, but indifferent about loving difficult people."[6]

Only with love can knowledge be used according to the "more excellent way" to protect and build up the church (Eph. 4:11–16).

Without Love
Risk-Taking Faith Is Worthless

The third spiritual gift Paul presents is faith (1 Cor. 12:9). He imagines himself possessing the most excellent gift of faith imaginable, "so as to remove mountains." Like Abraham, he would believe God for the impossible and actively trust him to do miraculous works. He would be a powerhouse of prayer, a spiritual risk taker, a virtual George Müller,[7] greatly admired and sought by all. He would be a courageous David racing out in battle to kill the Philistine giant Goliath (1 Sam. 17:32). But even with such a powerful spiritual gift, if love is not present, the gift becomes a means of glorifying oneself rather than serving others.

Some "miracle" workers on television may claim to do the impossible by faith, but they talk more about money, success, and themselves than about the people they supposedly help. Like the self-flaunting Pharisees, they want to "be seen by others" (Matt. 6:5). They love the praise of man and want to be revered as spiritual giants who do great things for God. They use their wonderful gifts to promote themselves, not the body of Christ.

> "Too often Christians are concerned about hidden truth, but indifferent about loving difficult people."
> —George Sweeting

I recall a radio preacher who spoke often of the marvelous things God was doing through his broadcasts and how God miraculously provided funds without his begging for money (which can be a subtle way of begging for money). But those who knew the man personally and worked for him saw things differently. They saw a man who was obsessed with money and public image. They saw his gift of faith being used to guarantee his own financial security. They saw a man who didn't care much at all for people but who cared a lot about himself.

No wonder Paul declares so emphatically that such a powerful gift without love is worth "nothing." Paul means what he says. Without love he knew he would be spiritually fruitless rather than a spiritual powerhouse.

Without love, the Christian leader is on the wrong path of the Christian life. But when faith is combined with love, the body of Christ is built up and advances forward on the royal road, the "more excellent way" of love.

Without Love
Giving All One's Money to the Poor
Is Unprofitable

Paul next considers giving away all his worldly possessions—his home, property, furniture, savings, and all the things he cherishes most—to feed the poor. He gives it all and reduces himself to abject poverty. Surely this is the ultimate, altruistic action. Wouldn't such giving be, by definition, *love*? Not necessarily. Paul makes it clear that the most extraordinary, self-sacrificing action can be done without love.

Self-sacrifice can be done for self-interest as illustrated by Ananias and Sapphira in the book of Acts. This couple sold their property and gave money to the apostles to distribute to the poor (Acts 5:1–11). However, they gave without love. They weren't really concerned about the needs of the poor, but about themselves. They didn't love God or their neighbor. Like the trumpet-blowing Pharisees whom Jesus condemned in the Sermon on the Mount (Matt. 6:1–5), Ananias and Sapphira gave in order to enhance their personal prestige in the sight of the church. They gave to receive the praise of people. Their love was hypocritical love (Rom. 12:9). They gave to the poor, but without the true, inner motivating power of love, so their giving profited them nothing. Although they gave money to the poor, they were spiritually bankrupt, and God rejected their gift.

Paul says, therefore, that if he gave all he owned to the poor but did so apart from love, it would be unproductive, useless, worthless, and of no eternal value. Even after such sacrifice he would be a spiritually bankrupt man. He would not be humbly serving others, but would be serving himself.

In contrast, when one is moved by love to meet the needs of the poor, giving all of one's possessions profits everyone. Such is the love that motivated the Lord Jesus Christ to give up the riches of heaven and become poor for us. For that reason, "God has highly exalted him and bestowed on him the name that is above every name" (Phil. 2:9). Jesus gave according to the "more excellent way."

Without Love
the Ultimate Sacrifice of One's Life
Is Pointless

Finally, Paul envisions himself as the ultimate hero of the faith. In an act of supreme sacrifice, he surrenders his body to the painful flames of martyrdom for Christ. Such a sacrifice would certainly inspire other believers to faithfulness, greater dedication, and courage. It would provide a powerful witness of the gospel to nonbelievers. But Paul warns us that even suffering and martyrdom for Christ can be done for the wrong reasons.

Some people take great pride in suffering for their faith. For others, it is worth dying in order to be remembered as a hero of the faith. In the early years of Christianity, becoming a martyr became at times a means of achieving great fame. One historian comments, "It soon was clear to all Christians that extraordinary fame and honor attached to martyrdom."[8] Some martyrs, like Ignatius, were showered with adulations before their martyrdom. Not that Ignatius sought martyrdom for personal praise, but he illustrates that it could be a temptation to some to seek to be immortalized in the annals of church history as a martyr for Christ. It was said of Polycarp, who was burned alive, that his bones were "more valuable than precious stones and finer than refined gold" and his grave became a sacred place to gather.[9] Recognizing the potential for such adulation, Paul finds it necessary to say that offering up one's life apart from love is a worthless sacrifice, an empty religious show, a hollow performance.

When it is motivated by the welfare of others and the glory of Christ, however, martyrdom becomes the ultimate sacrifice of love. Jonathan

Edwards, in his book *Charity and Its Fruits,* summarizes God's perspective on love and self-sacrifice this way:

> [God] delights in little things when they spring from sincere love to himself. A cup of cold water given to a disciple in sincere love is worth more in God's sight than all one's goods given to feed the poor, yea, than the wealth of a kingdom given away, or a body offered up in the flames, without love.[10]

Only when martyrdom is the result of love for God and others is it the "more excellent way."

Divine Mathematics

Imagine for a moment what the Corinthians must have thought when they first heard Paul's words read publicly in the congregational meeting. They probably couldn't believe their ears! Paul's message was contrary to their entire way of thinking and behaving. They were deficient in love and they didn't even realize it! Their pride of knowledge and miraculous gifts had deceived them.

D. A. Carson, Bible commentator and professor of New Testament at Trinity Evangelical Divinity School, describes Paul's reasoning in this passage in terms of "divine mathematics." According to divine mathematics, "five minus one equals zero."[11] Or, as George Sweeting remarks, "gifts, minus love, equals zero."[12]

Author Jerry Bridges, giving a vivid illustration of divine mathematics, asks his readers to do this:

> Write down, either in your imagination or on a sheet of paper, a row of zeros. Keep adding zeros until you have filled a whole line on the page. What do they add up to? Exactly nothing! Even if you were to write a thousand of them, they would still be nothing. But put a positive number in front of them and immediately they have value. This is the way it is with our gifts and faith and zeal. They are the zeros on the page. Without love, they count for nothing. But put love in front of

them and immediately they have value. And just as the number two gives more value to a row of zeros than the number one does, so more and more love can add exponentially greater value to our gifts.[13]

Without love, our most extraordinary gifts and highest achievements are ultimately fruitless to the church and before God. In Paul's way of thinking, nothing has lasting spiritual value unless it springs from love.

A Modern Paraphrase

Picturing himself as the most extraordinary teacher or leader to ever live, Paul would say:

If I were the most gifted communicator to ever preach, so that millions of people were moved by my oratory, but didn't have love, I would be an annoying, empty wind-bag before God and people.

If I had the most charismatic personality, so that everyone was drawn to me like a powerful magnet, but didn't have Christlike love, I would be a phony, a dud.

If I were the greatest visionary leader the church has ever heard, but didn't have love, I would be misguided and lost.

If I were the bestselling author on theology and church growth, but didn't have love, I would be an empty-headed failure.

If I sacrificially gave all my waking hours to discipling future leaders, but did it without love, I would be a false guide and model.

Chapter 2

Patient and Kind

Love is patient and kind.
1 Corinthians 13:4

Imagine more than four hundred Christians from sixty different nations and various denominational backgrounds living together twenty-four hours a day. Imagine them working together in extremely tight quarters, most of them for two years, some for even longer. Imagine them doing all of this as unpaid volunteers! Such is life aboard the ship *Logos Hope*.

For nearly fifty years, Operation Mobilization's ships, including *Logos Hope*, have sailed around the world stopping at ports in more than 150 countries. Serving as a Christian bookfair and conference center, the ships have welcomed more than forty-seven million people on board. The ships are the result of the vision of George Verwer, founder of Operation Mobilization (known as OM). OM was one of the first short-term mission organizations and has trained thousands of people in missions.

The volunteers who serve on the ships are ordinary people. They have the same weaknesses and character flaws as other human beings. They experience the same difficulties people experience ashore. The only difference is that on the ships there is no running away from conflict. How can they live and work together under such extreme conditions without destroying one another? The answer: love.

From the very start of OM, George Verwer preached that without a "revolution of love"[1] the vision for the ships and for the thousands of short-term literature teams would be an impossible dream. The kind of love necessary for working together on these ships is not a sentimental, fluffy love. It is Calvary's selfless, self-sacrificing love. It is the kind of love described

in 1 Corinthians 13:4–7: love that is patient and kind, love that does not
envy or boast, is not arrogant or rude, does not insist on its own way, and
is not irritable or resentful. It is Christlike love.

Instructions, Not Poetry

First Corinthians 13 is not a theoretical discourse on love or a flowery hymn
glorifying the feelings of love. Paul was not a romantic poet. He was an
apostle of Jesus Christ—a global missionary, church planter, pastor, and
teacher. These words are a critical part of his instruction and correction to
the church at Corinth, which was being torn apart by loveless behavior.

In order to help the Corinthians understand their own deficiencies and
the "more excellent way," Paul lists fifteen positive and negative descriptions
of love. In the Greek text, all of these descriptions are verbs describing what
love does and doesn't do. In English, these descriptions are often translated
as adjectives.

Love is
   1. patient (= longsuffering, forbearing)
   2. kind

Love is *not*
   3. envious   Love delights in the successes of others
   4. boastful   Love promotes and praises others
   5. arrogant   Love is humble and modest
   6. rude   Love promotes proper decorum
   7. selfish   Love is self-sacrificing
   8. easily angered   Love is calm and slow to anger
   9. resentful   Love forgives
 10. joyful over evil   11. Love rejoices with the truth

Love
 12. bears all things
 13. believes all things
 14. hopes all things
 15. endures all things

These fifteen qualities beautifully portray the character and behavior of the Lord Jesus Christ. We are to pattern our love and leadership after him (1 John 2:6). With Christ living and working within us through the Holy Spirit, the same behaviors should be true of us—whether we are elders, pastors, deacons, youth workers, Sunday school teachers, music directors, missionaries, evangelists, Bible study leaders, or church administrators.

In our ministry with people, these qualities should be uppermost in our mind. One of the most important chapters in the Bible for life in the local church and for Christian leadership is 1 Corinthians 13. It defines how we should behave in marriage, friendship, church, and society. It describes what our character should be like—and *in Christian ministry, character is everything.*

Paul didn't just write pretty words about love, he lived them, and the Corinthians saw the truth of these words in his life.

Love Is Patient

If we were to ask our Lord, "What is a loving Christian leader like?" he would first answer, "Patient and kind." So Paul begins and ends his love catalog with the patient, enduring nature of love (1 Cor. 13:4, 7). In an imperfect world, a leader must be characterized by patience.

The Greek verb for patience denotes "longsuffering" or "forbearance," particularly in respect to personal injuries or wrongs suffered. The Christian spirit of love does not seek to retaliate. It is not quick to anger.

God himself is the supreme example of longsuffering.[2] When we are tempted to be impatient with others, we should stop and think about the gracious longsuffering of God with us and our many wrongs against him. In light of his patience toward us, who are we to think that we cannot patiently bear with the weaknesses and failures of others—or the wrongs they may have done to us?

> **God himself is the supreme example of longsuffering.**

Lack of patience is a serious deficiency in a Christian leader. Our work with people is primarily a spiritual work, so it must be done God's way, with great patience and care. An impatient leader is as destructive to people as an impatient father is to his children or as an impatient shepherd is to his sheep.

Patience is needed because life is full of frustrations, hurts, and injustices. In fact, it is impossible to lead people without eventually being attacked. People will assail their leaders' character, criticize their decisions, speak evil behind their backs, and take advantage of their love.

In response to such attacks, love suffers long. So Paul instructs the Lord's servant to be patient when wronged:

> And the Lord's servant must not be quarrelsome but kind to everyone, able to teach, patiently enduring evil, correcting his opponents with gentleness. God may perhaps grant them repentance leading to a knowledge of the truth, and they may escape from the snare of the devil, after being captured by him to do his will. (2 Tim. 2:24–26)

Also, patience is needed when dealing with people's many weaknesses and failures. We must have patience to bear with those who are slow to learn, resistant to change, weak in faith, quick to complain, forgetful of their responsibilities, emotionally unstable, fearful, or wayward. Paul teaches that we are to "admonish the idle, encourage the fainthearted, help the weak, *be patient with them all*" (1 Thess. 5:14; italics added). Also, Paul instructs Timothy: "preach the word ... reprove, rebuke, and exhort, *with complete patience*" (2 Tim. 4:2; italics added).

Lack of patience is a serious deficiency in a Christian leader. An impatient leader is as destructive to people as an impatient father is to his children or as an impatient shepherd is to his sheep.

Patient Leaders in Action

Being patient doesn't imply passivity or a refusal to confront people's sins or problems. Without his patient pastoral leadership, Paul and the Corinthians would have gone their separate ways. Instead, his firm yet patient handling of the problems preserved the relationship. When the Corinthians unjustly criticized him, Paul didn't give up on them, cut them off, become vindictive, return evil for evil, or express anger in a sinful way. Instead, he answered their criticisms, confronted their sins, and warned of discipline. What is even more remarkable is that he did so with true patience and heartfelt love.

Paul, therefore, could say to the Corinthians that his leadership was marked by patience, kindness, and love:

> We put no obstacle in anyone's way, so that no fault may be found with our ministry, but as servants of God we commend ourselves in every way ... [by] patience, kindness, the Holy Spirit, genuine love. (2 Cor. 6:3–4, 6)

Patience is just as important in church leadership today as it was in Paul's day. The life of Robert C. Chapman provides us with one of the most inspiring and challenging examples of Spirit-filled patience in the face of church struggles and contentious people. You can read about this remarkable man in the booklet *Agape Leadership: Lessons in Spiritual Leadership from the Life of R. C. Chapman.*[3]

The Amazing Life of Robert C. Chapman

Robert Chapman was well known for his love. And like all loving leaders, he showed extraordinary patience with difficult people and their problems. Apart from the Bible, no one has influenced my thinking about love and leadership more than Robert Chapman.

In his day, some called Chapman an "apostle of love," and Charles Haddon Spurgeon referred to him as "the saintliest man I ever knew." He was the spiritual mentor to George Müller, the founder and director of the world-famous Ashley Down Orphanage in Bristol, England. Chapman was also a close friend to Hudson Taylor, and one of the first trustees of Taylor's China Inland Mission.

Robert Chapman left his profession as a lawyer in London to become pastor of a small Particular Baptist church in Barnstaple, England. This contentious little congregation had gone through three different pastors in the eighteen months prior to Chapman's arrival. He was sure to become the fourth pastor to be dismissed.

The story of how Chapman completely turned around this fighting church by his Spirit-filled forbearance, love, and Bible teaching ministry is an inspiring account of Christlike leadership. The church eventually became a large, harmonious church. It was known throughout England for its amazing love, missionary outreach, and compassionate ministries to the poor.

By the end of his life, at age ninety-nine, Chapman had become so well known for his loving disposition and wisdom that a letter from abroad addressed simply to "R. C. Chapman, University of Love, England," was correctly delivered to his home. Chapman demonstrated the "more excellent way" of patient, loving leadership.

Love Is Kind

Paul's first two descriptions of love are paired together and balance each other perfectly: Love suffers long (the passive quality) and love shows kindness (the active quality). Patience and kindness are two sides of the same coin of love. "You can no more have love without kindness than you can have springtime without flowers," writes W. Graham Scroggie.[4]

Kindness is a readiness to do good, to help, to relieve burdens, to be useful, to serve, to be tender, and to be sympathetic to others. It has been said, "Kindness is love in work clothes."

God is kind to all,[5] and the work of our Lord Jesus Christ on earth demonstrated abundant and compassionate kindness. The gospels are replete with stories of his kindness to needy men and women: Jesus touched a man, whom Luke the physician described as "full of leprosy" (Luke 5:12–13). William Lane accurately describes this as "an unheard-of act of compassion."[6] When Jesus encountered a deformed woman bent over by disease and a demonic agent, "he laid his hands on her" (Luke 13:13). He touched the eyes of the blind and fed the multitudes. He made time to stop and bless little children. Jesus ate and talked with the most hated people of his day, the tax collectors. A notoriously immoral woman found kindness and mercy at his feet (Luke 7:37–50). Acts 10:38 sums up the work of Jesus this way: "He went about doing good."

If we want to reach and influence people for Jesus Christ, we must cultivate a kindly disposition.

The Power of Kindness

Scripture insists that all those who lead and teach the Lord's people are servants who must be kind to everyone (2 Tim. 2:24). "As servants of God," Paul writes, "we commend ourselves in every way" by patience and kindness (2 Cor. 6:4, 6).

Augustine, in his book *Confessions,* describes how even during his unconverted days, the renowned preacher and bishop, Ambrose, moved him more by kindness than even by excellent preaching:

> That "man of God" received me like a father and expressed pleasure at my coming with a kindness most fitting in a bishop. I began to like him, at first indeed not as a teacher of the truth, for I had absolutely no confidence in your Church, but as a human being who was kind to me.[7]

Loving leaders are kind, even to people who criticize, antagonize, or oppose them. It was said of Thomas Cranmer, an archbishop of the Church of England: "To do him any wrong was to beget a kindness from him."[8]

Leadership without kindness is a disaster. The Old Testament account of King Rehoboam, Solomon's son, for example, illustrates how unkindness ruined a king. Before Rehoboam was coronated, the people of Israel came to him and demanded to know the spirit in which he would rule them because his father's rule ended in harsh oppression. Before answering the people, he rightly consulted with the elders—experienced men who had served his father and knew good and bad leadership principles. They counseled Rehoboam to lead with a kindly disposition. They said, "If you will be good [kind] to this people and please them and speak good words to them, then they will be your servants forever" (2 Chron. 10:7).

Disregarding the wisdom and experience of these older men, Rehoboam rejected their counsel. He foolishly chose the counsel of his young, inexperienced friends to treat the people with a harsh, heavy hand (2 Chron. 10:10–11). As a result, the nation divided in civil war. The people wanted a kind king, not a harsh one. And people are no different today. Kindness is a key to leading people effectively.

If we want to reach and influence people for Jesus Christ, we must cultivate a kindly disposition. Acts of kindness impact people in big ways and capture their attention: a card sent to one who is sick, a concerned phone call, an invitation to dinner, a readiness to help relieve a burden, a caring voice, a gentle touch, a thoughtful gesture, a simple expression of interest in another's concerns, a visit. The way of kindness is the "more excellent way."

Chapter 3

Not Envious or Boastful

Love does not envy or boast.
1 Corinthians 13:4

On Paul's second missionary journey he traveled to the city of Corinth, where he stayed for eighteen months (Acts 18:11). Corinth at the time was a prosperous Roman colony, and Paul viewed it as a strategic city for the advancement of the gospel. It was a miniature Rome, a booming, wealthy commercial center. Corinth could offer its citizens and travelers all the pleasures of a free-minded, cosmopolitan city. People in that culture valued success through wealth, personal status seeking, competitive individualism, wisdom, and knowledge. This value system not only permeated the culture but also adversely influenced the church. According to one commentator, "The problem was not that the church was in Corinth but that too much of Corinth was in the church."[1]

When Paul wrote 1 Corinthians some three and a half years after leaving that city, he had to address serious problems within the congregation. At the root of these problems were the worldly attitudes and beliefs that were inherently hostile to the gospel of the cross of Christ and its wisdom.

As a result of numerous sins in the church, Paul is compelled to take a negative tack, describing eight character qualities that are inconsistent with love. These eight qualities—all betraying a sinful lack of love—divided the church at Corinth just as they divide churches today.

Paul plainly states that love is *not*:

1. envious
2. boastful

3. arrogant
4. rude
5. selfish
6. easily angered
7. resentful
8. joyful over evil (rejoices with the truth)

These eight vices are totally incompatible with love. In brief, they express the self-centered life that tears apart relationships and spoils the unity that should characterize every local church. Paul's list serves as an objective standard to correct our selfish behaviors and to guide us on the "more excellent way."

Love Is Not Envious

Topping Paul's list is a vice that has wrecked countless relationships and split many churches—envy or jealousy. Jealousy divided the church at Corinth, and it belied the Corinthians' empty boast of being spiritual people: "For while there is jealousy and strife among you, are you not of the flesh and behaving only in a human way?" (1 Cor. 3:3).

Envy is totally incompatible with love. It destroys love, and with it a leader's character.

Envy makes one resentful of others' good fortune. It covets others' gifts, possessions, or positions of influence. It is suspicious and critical of another's popularity. Nathaniel Vincent pointedly expresses the tormenting, selfish spirit of envy:

How much of hell is there in the temper of an envious man! The happiness of another is his misery, the good of another is his affliction. He looks upon the virtue of another with an evil eye, and is as sorry at the praise of another as if that praise were taken away from himself. Envy makes him a hater of his neighbor, and his own tormentor.[2]

Envy is totally incompatible with love. It destroys love—and with it, a leader's character.

Envy Is Destructive

The account of King Saul and David provides a vivid illustration of the destructive power of envy in a leader's life. Initially Saul loved David, but almost immediately after the shepherd boy's stunning victory over the giant Goliath, the king became envious of him.

There was much to envy about David. He was young, handsome, strong, brilliant, talented, and popular. A successful warrior, he was abundantly blessed by God in all that he did, and "his name was highly esteemed" (1 Sam. 18:30). He was so popular and greatly admired that the women sang, "Saul has struck down his thousands, and David his ten thousands" (1 Sam. 18:7).

This comparison of Saul's victories with David's greater achievements enraged the king and stirred up the vilest passions of jealousy. He came to hate David and opposed him at every turn. He spoke evil against him at every opportunity and thought only of David's downfall. Rather than repent of his envy and seek God's help in acknowledging David as God's gift to the nation, Saul gave full vent to his sin. His envy led to discontentment, paranoid thinking, personal misery, and murderous scheming. In the end, Saul destroyed himself and lost his kingdom. His life proved that where there is envy and jealousy there is not love.

None of us are immune from petty, self-centered envy. Even the most committed missionaries and servants of the Lord have struggled with this sin. George Müller was the founder of the Ashley Down orphanage in Bristol, England. While co-pastoring with Henry Craik at a church in Bristol, England, George Müller saw that people enjoyed the other man's teaching more than his own. Henry Craik was not only an excellent Bible teacher, but he was also a first-rate classical and Hebrew scholar. Unlike King Saul, however, Müller was a man of extraordinary faith and prayer. He confessed his envious feelings toward his co-worker and confronted his sin:

> When in the year 1832, I saw how some preferred my beloved friend's ministry to my own, I determined, in the strength of God, to rejoice in this, instead of envying him. I said, with John the Baptist, "A man can receive nothing, except it be given him from heaven" (John 3:27). This resisting the devil hindered separation of heart.[3]

George Müller's and Henry Craik's friendship lasted for thirty-six years, until Craik died.[4] Although both were strong, multi-gifted men with quite different personalities, their long relationship was a public testimony to the power of Christian love. Müller was well known for his many lifelong friendships with people like Hudson Taylor, Charles Spurgeon, D. L. Moody, Robert Chapman, and others. Envious people, unfortunately, have few real friends and many conflicts.

We need to be aware that envy is a prevalent sin among the Lord's people and Christian leaders. Pastors can go to bizarre extremes to eliminate from the church gifted people who threaten them. Churches can envy other churches that are larger or are growing rapidly. Missionaries can envy other missionaries who are more fruitful or better supported. Bible study leaders can envy more popular Bible study leaders; singers can envy other singers who sing more often or receive louder applause; elders can envy fellow elders who shine brighter in leadership ability or knowledge; and deacons can envy fellow deacons who serve more effectively or are sought out for help more frequently.

Love Delights in the Successes of Others

Love "does not burn with envy."[5] Love is large-hearted, other-oriented, content, and full of good will toward others. "When love sees someone who is popular, successful, beautiful, or talented, it is glad for them and never jealous or envious."[6] Brotherly love tries to "outdo one another in showing honor" (Rom. 12:10).

The loving Barnabas, Paul's co-worker, for example, rejoiced over Paul's greater giftedness and invited him into significant ministry opportunities as a co-laborer teaching in the church at Antioch (Acts 11:19–26). The loving Jonathan, King Saul's son, differed greatly from his envious father. He admired and valued David's leadership abilities. He was willing to jeopardize his own future role as a king (1 Sam. 23:16–17) in order to protect and promote David's cause.

As Christian leaders, our commitment to love should prompt us to consciously rejoice over the successes and talents of others. We should seek to advance the ministry opportunities available to others and treat their strengths and gifts as if they were our own (1 Cor. 12:25–26). When feelings of envy toward others arise, we must confess those feelings for what they are—sin and self-centeredness. Like George Müller, we must be determined, in the strength of God, to rejoice in the other person's success. We will be happier and more content, and God will be pleased when we think and act according to the "more excellent way."

Love Does Not Boast

Like the sin of envy, boasting, or bragging, is a sinful preoccupation with oneself. Braggarts crave attention. They want others to praise their abilities, knowledge, successes, and even their sufferings for God. Because they desire recognition, they speak too highly and too much of themselves, although they may have nothing significant to say.

Boasting has long been a serious problem among religious people. The sanctimonious, trumpet-blowing Pharisees shamelessly craved the attention of people. They were religious show-offs. Jesus pointed out how they loved the front seats in the synagogue, respectful greetings on the street, and praise for their public acts of piety. Likewise, believers in the church at Corinth boasted about their superior wisdom, their favorite teacher's speaking skills, and their extraordinary spiritual experiences. They were full of themselves, not full of love.

Such boasting is still a problem today. I clearly remember a missionary evangelist who came to my home, along with others, for dinner. For three hours he never stopped talking about himself, his ministries, and his success. He told us how hard he worked, how far and wide he traveled, and how blessed he was of God. Not once, however, during the long evening meal did he inquire about others at the table. He was a boaster.

Another time I was at a church conference that had hundreds of book and ministry exhibits. Our book table was next to a ministry booth featuring an internationally known pastor and author. The entire time he was at his booth he talked nonstop about himself. We couldn't help but overhear him praise himself for two full days. He told every person he talked to how large his church was, how many people were on his staff, and how large the church budget was. He wasn't even subtle about dropping the names of the famous people he knew and places he had preached. He was a braggart.

Boasting, however, helps no one. We speak of "empty boasting," but in fact, as Scroggie says, "There is no other kind of boasting. The very nature and essence of a boast is emptiness. Boasting is always an advertisement of poverty."[7] Boasting does not build up or serve the church community. Boasting does not honor Christ. Rather, it intimidates and it divides people. It provokes others to envy. Boasting is particularly abhorrent in a leader. It mars a leader's character. We wouldn't want people in the church to follow such an example. Braggarts blatantly disregard God's prohibition against self-praise: "Let another praise you, and not your own mouth; a stranger, and not your own lips" (Prov. 27:2).

Braggarts build themselves up, jealous people tear others down, but loving people build others up.

Love Promotes and Praises Others

Love promotes and praises others. It is self-effacing and shies away from speaking of itself. So those who are possessed of Christ's love delight in focusing attention on others, in pushing others to center stage, and in sharing the spotlight of attention.

In the context of thinking about spiritual giftedness, Paul writes, "I say to everyone among you not to think of himself more highly than he ought to think, but to think with sober judgment" (Rom. 12:3). This doesn't imply that we never talk about ourselves or allow others to inquire about our interests or ministries. There's a fine line between speaking about ourselves in a non-boastful way and boasting in a sinful, self-centered way. Like Paul and Barnabas, missionaries need to report on God's work through their labors to those who support them (Acts 14:27; 15:3). Skillful teachers often use illustrations taken from their personal experiences to communicate effectively

Braggarts build themselves up, jealous people tear others down, but loving people build others up.

without boasting (Gal. 2:1–14). The difference is that braggarts use people to fulfill their own need for attention and praise.

A missionary friend on the way back to Africa found himself on board a ship with the young Billy Graham and witnessed love that does not brag. Graham was on his way to the London Crusade. As the two men met and talked together during their voyage, something about Graham touched my friend deeply. Graham asked questions about my friend's life and ministry in Africa; he was genuinely interested in his work. My friend particularly observed that Graham rarely spoke about himself or his phenomenal experiences as an evangelist. At the end of their voyage, the missionary asked the young evangelist how he could pray for him, and the answer was, "Pray that I will be a humble man." That prayer many years ago reflected a heart of wisdom and love. Decades later it is apparent that pride of gift or success is not a criticism that has been leveled against Billy Graham.

> "Boasting is always an advertisement of poverty."
> —W. Graham Scroggie

There is something to learn from his example. *Humble people are not self-absorbed braggarts.* Instead, they promote and praise others according to the "more excellent way" of love.

Chapter 4

Not Arrogant or Rude

Love ... is not arrogant or rude.
1 Corinthians 13:4–5

Hardly anything is more contrary to the example of Christ, the message of the cross, and Christian love than arrogant self-importance. Christians are sinners saved by God's grace, and all of our spiritual gifts and ministries have been graciously given to us by God. Thus the Scripture says, "What do you have that you did not receive? If then you received it, why do you boast as if you did not receive it?" (1 Cor. 4:7).

There is no place whatsoever for egotism in the Lord's work, especially for those who lead and teach the community of the cross. Yet arrogance is a widely recognized problem among leaders today.

During a seminary graduation ceremony I attended, the president of the seminary delivered a challenging message entitled "Big-Shot Syndrome." It was gratifying to hear him warn the graduating students against thinking too highly of themselves and acting like big shots rather than humble servants of Jesus Christ. To bring his point home, he had cut a towel into small squares and put them in a basket. At the end of his message he invited the graduates to come forward to receive a small piece of towel. He then suggested that they place the piece of towel in their wallets to continually remind them that Jesus Christ took a towel and humbly washed his disciples' feet. What an excellent reminder to those young servants of the gospel. Remembering Christ's example of humility is good for anyone who serves in local church leadership.

Love Is Not Arrogant

An arrogant spirit permeated the church at Corinth, and this generated many of its problems.[1] Arrogance is contrary to love because it focuses on self more than others. Arrogant people, especially religious ones, think they are better than other people. They think they know a lot more than they actually do, they consider themselves holier than others, and they imagine themselves more gifted than they really are. They are blind to their own glaring sins, personal weaknesses, and doctrinal errors. As Amy Carmichael once said, "Those who think too much of themselves don't think enough."[2]

> "Nothing sets a Christian so much out of the devil's reach than humility."
>
> —Jonathan Edwards

The Greek word for *arrogant* can be literally rendered "puffed up" or "inflated." J. B. Phillips captures the idea well in his translation: Love does not "cherish inflated ideas of its own importance."[3] In other words, love doesn't have a superiority complex. This was an important concept for Jesus' disciples to understand because many of the religious leaders of their day were puffed up with religious pride. One self-inflated Pharisee was observed praying to himself: "God, I thank you that I am not like other men" (Luke 18:11).

In contrast, Jesus strictly prohibited his disciples from any kind of idolatrous self-exaltation: "The greatest among you shall be your servant. Whoever exalts himself will be humbled, and whoever humbles himself will be exalted" (Matt. 23:11–12). Humility of mind, not arrogance, is to be the badge of Christ's followers. Arrogance is the disposition of the devil (Isa. 14:13–14), not of Christ. And, as Jonathan Edwards wisely observed, "Nothing sets a Christian so much out of the devil's reach than humility."[4]

A New Testament example of an arrogant, big-shot church leader is Diotrephes. The Bible says he loved to be "first." John writes:

> I have written something to the church, but Diotrephes, who likes to put himself first, does not acknowledge our authority. So if I come, I will bring up what he is doing, talking wicked nonsense against us. And not content with that, he refuses to welcome the brothers, and also stops those who want to and puts them out of the church. (3 John 9–10)

Diotrephes was so puffed up with himself he criticized and refused to listen to the beloved apostle John. He abused people who disagreed with him, created an atmosphere of fear within the local church, and demanded his own way. He was not a builder of people but a limiter of people. He was not a uniter but a divider. He was not a humble-minded servant leader. He would not share the ministry with peers and colleagues such as Paul. He refused godly correction and instruction. His heart was not contrite before God, and his arrogant spirit divided people and hurt the church. In Paul's words, Diotrephes was "a noisy gong or a clanging cymbal" (1 Cor. 13:1).

Love Is Humble and Modest

The nature of love is the opposite of arrogance. Love thinks humbly and modestly about self and others (Rom. 12:3). The spirit of love says, "Do not be haughty, but associate with the lowly. Never be wise in your own sight" (Rom. 12:16). Peter exhorted the church elders to "clothe yourselves, all of you, with humility" (1 Peter 5:5). Paul reminded the Ephesian elders that he served "the Lord with all humility" (Acts 20:19).

Humility is the mindset of a servant. It makes a leader more teachable, more receptive to constructive criticism, better able to work with others, better qualified to deal with other people's failures and sins, more willing to submit to others, less prone to fight, and quicker to reconcile differences. Without humility, one cannot be a Christlike leader (Matt. 11:29; Phil. 2:7–8).

Humility also makes teachers of the Word better able to relate to people at all levels of life, even the poorest and least educated, as did our Lord Jesus Christ. Teachers of God's Word must be humble servants or they contradict the message of the Bible.

Paul and Apollos were highly gifted leaders and teachers. They could easily have been tempted to be puffed up with feelings of superiority because of their brilliant minds and many successes in the gospel. Yet Paul wisely reminds the Corinthians, who prized big-shot teachers, that he and Apollos were humble servants of the Lord, nothing more. He writes, "What then is Apollos? What is Paul? Servants through whom you believed, as the Lord assigned to each [of us]" (1 Cor. 3:5).

Loving leaders and teachers, then, are humble and modest. They do not treat people arrogantly, but respectfully. They humbly serve and lift up others, not themselves.

C. S. Lewis, one of the world's best-known Christian authors, was a humble man who as a teacher lived out the "more excellent way" of love. Lewis taught at Oxford and Cambridge Universities in England and became internationally famous when he converted from atheism to Christianity. He wrote many Christian books that have sold in the millions and been translated into many languages. His writings have touched countless lives for Jesus Christ.

Despite enormous worldwide success, Lewis was a humble man and a teacher of both scholars and children, and available to all kinds of people who sought his advice. He personally answered thousands of letters from ordinary people he had never met but who asked for his help. Lewis believed God wanted him to answer every letter, which he did, and "he treated each correspondent as if he or she were as important as the king or queen of England."[5] This is a remarkable accomplishment given his demanding schedule. He answered people's questions about depression, marital conflict, and difficult theological problems. He also committed himself to praying daily for many troubled people worldwide who requested his prayers—people he never met and some who were quite eccentric.

Lewis (an Anglican) attended the local Anglican church near his home, where he related to a diverse group of people, some of whom had little realization of his literary success or worldwide popularity. Since heaven would be filled with all kinds of people worshiping God, Lewis considered it "unthinkable" to seek a church with a membership made up only of academic and scholarly types. Worshiping at his local church was, for him, preparation for heavenly worship.[6]

His humble attitude toward others is revealed in a delightful story told by his taxi driver, Clifford Morris. (Lewis didn't own a car.) Lewis treated him, as he did everyone, with caring and attentive respect. One of C. S. Lewis's biographers, Lyle W. Dorsett, writes:

> [Morris] found Mr. Lewis to be warm and congenial, always treating
> him as an equal despite the wide disparity between their social classes
> and educational levels. This treatment surprised and blessed Morris,

because other men—including Christians—were never so generous. Occasionally, Professor Lewis would get into the car and on the way to Cambridge say, "Morris, I'm sorry I can't talk for a quarter of an hour. I need to do my prayers."[7]

C. S. Lewis keenly understood the necessity of humility for Christian living and the many dangers of sinful pride. Of pride he wrote, "It was through Pride that the devil became the devil: Pride leads to every other vice: it is the complete anti-God state of mind."[8]

Those who live by the "more excellent way," however, don't suffer from an "anti-God state of mind." Instead, like their Savior, they are "gentle and lowly in heart" (Matt. 11:29).

Love Is Not Rude

Christlike love is to influence all behaviors, and Scripture tells us that love is not rude; it does not "behave with ill-mannered impropriety."[9] The verb for "rude" conveys the idea of acting disgracefully, contrary to established standards of proper conduct and decency. Thus inappropriate dress, inconsiderate talk, disregard for other people's time or moral conscience, taking advantage of people, tactlessness, ignoring the contributions and ideas of others, running roughshod over other's plans and interests, inappropriate behavior with the opposite sex, basic discourtesy and rudeness, and a general disregard for proper social conduct are all evidence of a lack of love and have no place in the local church.

A lack of love was evident in the rude behavior of the church at Corinth. Richer members didn't wait for poorer ones to arrive for the Lord's Supper. Instead, they selfishly ate their own expensive foods and left little food for the poor to eat (1 Cor. 11:21–22, 33).

Other members thoughtlessly used their so-called superior knowledge and liberties to trample over the consciences of their weaker brothers and sisters. They ate foods offered to pagan idols (1 Cor. 8), which created confusion and caused some believers to violate their conscience. During congregational meetings, certain gifted speakers were monopolizing the time and hindering others from expressing their spiritual gifts. Then there were those who interrupted while others were speaking. Some spoke in tongues without interpretation so the people didn't know what was being said. To put an end to their ill-mannered impropriety, Paul instructed that "all things should be done decently and in order" (1 Cor. 14:40).

Rudeness did not die out with the church in Corinth but characterizes our day as well. During a worship service in a church I was visiting, two young people in back of me were disgracefully disrupting the celebration of the Lord's Supper. They crunched on nuts and hard candies. They gulped water from plastic bottles, and every time they took a drink, the plastic water bottle popped. They whispered to one another and said "amen" along with the congregation, but only in mockery. They disturbed everyone around them.

After the service, I spoke to one of the church leaders about their behavior. He sighed in frustration. He assured me that they had tried to address the problem on other occasions, but that the parents refused correction. They felt their children had a right to eat and drink during the service. Of course, this kind of behavior isn't allowed in a movie theatre, but the parents thought it acceptable in church. They were rude, unloving people who had no regard for others.

Rudeness is not limited to age or social class. Intellectuals and highly educated people can be just as rude and thoughtless as anyone. At a Christian university, a conservative scholar presented a lecture on an unpopular, politically incorrect subject. As he spoke, the audience of scholars and leaders booed, hissed, and laughed at the speaker. This disgraceful display of rudeness with no regard for the speaker's feelings or beliefs was a far cry from love. Love is not rude.

We must resist the acceptance of rude behavior.

Love Promotes Proper Decorum

Loving people are considerate of how their behavior affects others, even in little things. Those who are possessed of God's love are sensitive to proper social relationships, public decency, social convention, politeness, tact, and proper conduct in dress, speech, and action. They are sensitive to the fact that people in certain churches would be upset if a preacher or song leader didn't wear a tie and jacket but wore jeans and a sweatshirt. They recognize that it would be inappropriate for a female Sunday school teacher to come to class dressed in clothes appropriate for the beach (1 Tim. 2:9–10). They would know better than to talk on a cell phone during a public church meeting.

Love recognizes that ill-mannered, rude behavior disrupts elder and deacon meetings (and all other committee meetings). Love fosters effective meetings in which all things are done properly and in an orderly fashion (1 Cor. 14:40). Talking over people, not listening, ignoring other people's ideas, making cutting comments and threats, bullying, and showing disrespect to those who disagree does not exemplify love. Such behavior has no place in church leadership.

As Western societies become more coarse and thoughtless of basic standards of courtesy and social decency, we must resist the acceptance of rude behavior. If not, it will have a harmful, degrading effect on our lives and on our churches.

This is an especially important issue to Christians who travel to other countries for Jesus Christ. Hudson Taylor was one of the greatest Christian leaders of all times, and he was acknowledged to be a loving leader. The remarkable story of his life and the founding of the China Inland Mission has been extensively documented.[10] One of Taylor's many leadership strengths was his ability to relate well to the Chinese because of his keen sense of propriety and his cultural sensitivity. At one time he complained in a letter about the lack of tact and—in effect, disrespect—some missionaries displayed toward Chinese customs and protocol, which are an important element of Chinese culture. His words should be heeded today:

> **"In nothing do we fail more, as a Mission, than in lack of tact and politeness."**
> **—Hudson Taylor**

> Some persons seem really clever in doing the right thing in the worst possible way, or at the most unfortunate time. Really dull, or rude persons will seldom be out of hot water in China; and though earnest and clever and pious will not effect much. In nothing do we fail more, as a Mission, than in lack of tact and politeness.[11]

Christ's Great Commission (Matt. 28:18–20) has given all Christians a global mission. Paul recognized this. A man of three different cultures— Jewish, Roman, and Greek—Paul, the evangelist, traveled extensively for the gospel and knew how to adapt properly to various social mores (1 Cor. 9:19–23; 10:32–33). We also, when we travel for Christ, need to be sensitive not to offend the societal conventions of our host nation but to be good ambassadors of God's love to all people.

Following the more excellent way of love means being keenly aware of what is considered tactful and polite in other cultures and being respectful of different people's social customs.

Chapter 5

Not Selfish or Easily Angered

Love … does not insist on its own way; it is not irritable.
1 Corinthians 13:4–5

The Bible doesn't hide the fact that even among the apostles, selfish attitudes and power struggles existed. James and John, for example, thinking exclusively of themselves, asked Jesus to give them places of highest honor in the kingdom: "Grant us to sit, one at your right hand and one at your left, in your glory" (Mark 10:37). James and John were "card-carrying members of the 'self-seekers' club."[1] Their request immediately sparked conflict among the other disciples, as selfish ambition always does. Mark records that "when the ten heard it, they began to be indignant at James and John" (Mark 10:41). They became indignant because they, too, were self-seekers and craved positions of power and glory for themselves.

This incident shows how little they understood their Lord's ways and how much they had yet to learn about loving and serving one another as brothers. "James and John want to sit on thrones in power and glory," writes John Stott; "Jesus knows that he must hang on a cross in weakness and shame. The antithesis is total."[2]

Love Is Not Selfish

The fifth negative statement aims at selfishness, the root of many of our problems, a vice totally incompatible with Christian love and leadership. Love, 1 Corinthians 13:5 states, "does not insist on its own way." This means that love does not seek its own interests or its own advantage. Love "is not preoccupied with the interest of the self."[3] This is especially important to understand because we live in an age of radical individualism. People in many modern Western societies are consumed with their own self-interest. They place themselves at the center of the universe, which is the rightful place of God. This all-consuming focus on self is completely contrary to Christian love.

If Jesus had sought his own advantage there would have been no cross. But the Scripture says, "Christ did not please himself" (Rom. 15:3). Our Lord came not to be served but to serve: "I am among you as the one who serves" (Luke 22:27).

Paul, too, did not seek his own way. If he had, he would never have endured all the grief involved in spreading the gospel and caring for the churches. But because of his love for Christ, expressed through love for others, he could say, "I try to please everyone in everything I do, not seeking my own advantage, but that of many" (1 Cor. 10:33). "For though I am free from all, I have made myself a servant to all" (1 Cor. 9:19). "I seek not what is yours but you.... I will most gladly spend and be spent for your souls" (2 Cor. 12:14–15).

This was not an easy example for the Corinthian believers to follow. In stark contrast, they insisted on their rights and freedoms to eat foods offered to pagan idols, even if taking such liberties hurt the conscience of their weaker brothers and sisters (1 Cor. 8–10). They didn't understand the spirit

"Christ did not please himself."
Rom. 15:3

of love that says, "If food makes my brother stumble, I will never eat meat, lest I make my brother stumble" (1 Cor. 8:13). It didn't matter to them that "if your brother is grieved by what you eat, you are no longer walking in love" (Rom. 14:15). They used their marvelous liberties and gifts for their own selfish ends rather than for the good of the whole community.

As self-seekers, they also didn't understand Christian ministry or the servant role of a Christian leader or teacher. Some at Corinth even viewed Paul's suffering and selfless life as an example of weakness and failure. Their view of Christian leadership was power and rulership, not weakness and servanthood; therefore, they doubted his apostleship. These same misconceptions about true Christian leadership persist today.

Love Is Self-Sacrificing

The great enemy of every shepherd is a selfish heart. A wonderful New Testament model of a loving leader and teacher is Barnabas. He was not a self-oriented throne seeker. Luke records that he was "a good man, full of the Holy Spirit and of faith" (Acts 11:24). Being full of the Holy Spirit, he was characterized by love (Gal. 5:22) and all the qualities of love described in 1 Corinthians 13:4–7.

> Barnabas thought more of what was best for the new church than his own prominence and security.

The first time we meet Barnabas in the New Testament he is selling land and giving the money to the poor saints in Jerusalem (Acts 4:36–37). Generosity toward others naturally flows out of love. As Robert Law says, "Love is the giving impulse."[4]

But what is most impressive about Barnabas is how he shared his leadership position and ministry with Paul. Barnabas had been sent by the leaders in Jerusalem to help with the newly established church in Antioch. It was an exciting place to be. God was doing new things among the Gentiles, and Barnabas was at the center of the action. Yet he thought more of what was best for the new church than his own prominence and security.

Believing that the church needed Paul's extraordinary giftedness, Barnabas traveled, at great personal sacrifice, to the city of Tarsus to find Paul and invite him to Antioch to teach. This meant Barnabas would be sharing his teaching and leadership role with Paul, who was far more gifted. Barnabas pushed Paul forward, and later Paul became the more prominent of the two. As one preacher aptly observed, "Barnabas was not a ministry hog." He didn't have to do all the ministering or get all the glory. Barnabas was not a throne seeker; he was a washer of feet (John 13:14). He was a lifter of people, not a limiter of people (Acts 11:19–24). He was a giver, not a taker. His love was the "giving variety," not the "getting variety."[5]

Barnabas was truly a loving Christian leader and teacher. He was not jealous of Paul, nor did he brag of his status as an apostle or of his own spirituality. He was not arrogant, rude, or selfish, but he gave himself for the benefit of others. No wonder the people called him "son of encouragement" (Acts 4:36; 11:23). He exemplified the motto: "Great things can happen when you don't care who gets the credit." Great things happened in the church at Antioch through Barnabas and Paul—and continue to happen in the church today—because of unselfish teachers and leaders.

A modern day Barnabas is John Stott, former rector of All Souls Church in London, honorary chaplain to the Queen of England, and author of many excellent biblical commentaries. A missions professor recounts that while walking through an airport, he saw an elderly man sitting in the airport chapel with a large pile of letters at his side, writing. It was John Stott. Like a loving shepherd, Stott wrote and encouraged many people, especially young people. And like Barnabas, John Stott is well known as a gracious servant of God who shared his teaching and leading ministry with others.[6]

Stott's lowly servant heart is illustrated by an account given by one of his Latin American colleagues who translated into Spanish for him while he was speaking in Cuba:

> … after I finished five days of translating for [John Stott], he invited me to do some birdwatching with him but I fell very ill. What a privilege it was to be fed, cared for, prayed over, comforted and affectionately ministered to by him. I have the impression that the chambermaids in the hotel where we stayed thought that I must be an extremely important person because I was being taken care of by a distinguished white, Anglo-Saxon gentleman—something they had never seen before.[7]

Loving leaders and teachers—whether Sunday school teachers or missionary evangelists—unselfishly give their time, energy, and possessions to help people. They put themselves out to serve others, they reach out to people in need, they are self-forgetful and ultimately self-renouncing. They don't belong to themselves and they are not concerned about being unfairly treated; they are not worried about being repaid or even properly thanked. They are godly people who look not only to their own interests, but also to the interests of others (Phil. 2:4).

Love Is Not Easily Provoked

A remarkable quality of love is that it is not easily provoked to an emotional state of anger. "It is not irritable." This is an eminently practical virtue for a leader. Leaders have to deal with a lot of difficult situations. There will always be plenty of fuel to provoke a leader to anger, irritability, offense, bitterness, and resentment. This is why one of the biblical qualifications for an elder is that he not be "quick-tempered" (Titus 1:7). Shepherds can't be kicking or killing the sheep because they are upset.

This doesn't mean that one never gets angry or irritated with people. The Bible doesn't say love does not get angry; it says love is not easily provoked to anger or irritation. There is righteous, controlled anger motivated by love and opposed to evil and falsehood that senselessly destroys people.[8] But love is not provoked in a destructive sense because of wrong motives. "The heart of man," says Jonathan Edwards, "is exceedingly prone to undue and sinful anger, being naturally full of pride and selfishness."[9] This anger is incompatible with love.

> "The heart of man is exceedingly prone to undue and sinful anger, being naturally full of pride and selfishness."
>
> **—Jonathan Edwards**

A seminary professor tells the story of being at a restaurant with a pastor when the server accidentally poured water over the pastor's suit. The pastor angrily snapped at the server, giving full vent to his displeasure. After cleaning up, the professor leaned over and whispered to the pastor, "Maybe we should witness to her of the love of Christ." The pastor got the message.

A loving heart (like Christ's) would immediately have felt compassion for the server and thought more of her feelings than of a soiled suit. It would have sought to ease the tension by downplaying the situation and reassuring the server. The incident could have easily been turned into a positive witness for Christ. Instead, the pastor thought only of himself and his suit. He was easily provoked.

Outside the church, such leaders misrepresent Christ and give his people a bad name in the world. And within the church, it is easy to see how those who are easily provoked to anger carelessly frighten, hurt, and divide people. They invite and accentuate conflict.

Angry people are focused not on others but on their own emotions and issues. When leaders are angry, problems are exaggerated, miscommunication and misunderstanding abound, and objectivity and reason disappear. When anger rules, small problems become big explosions that can blow a church to pieces. I am convinced that *much more damage is done to our churches by out-of-control anger than we care to admit.* It is a big problem.

The devil is a master at using anger to ruin churches and families, and he can often provoke godly leaders to do destructive things to others. None of us are immune from hurting people with our anger. Henry Drummond insightfully observes that anger is "the vice of the virtuous." Consider how quick we are to downplay and justify our angry outbursts toward others:

> We are inclined to look upon bad temper as a very harmless weakness.... And yet here, right in the heart of this analysis of love, it finds a place; and the Bible again and again returns to condemn it as one of the most destructive elements in human nature.
>
> *The peculiarity of ill temper is that it is the vice of the virtuous. It is often the one blot on an otherwise noble character.* You know men who are all but perfect, and women who would be entirely perfect, but for an easily ruffled, quick-tempered, or "touchy" disposition. The compatibility of ill temper with high moral character is one of the strangest and saddest problems of ethics[10] [italics added].

As Christians, when we face conflict and relational pain we are to be Spirit-controlled and self-controlled (Gal. 5:22–23). Out-of-control anger is the work of the flesh and the devil (Gal. 5:19–20; Eph. 4:30–32). There is an old saying that when you spill over a vase, what's inside is what comes out. When you are dealing with someone who is disagreeable or thoughtless, or who simply sees things differently than you do, what comes out of *you*? Take this matter seriously before the Lord and guard yourself from any self-justification.[11] The Scripture says, "Let every person be ... slow to anger; for the anger of man does not produce the righteousness of God" (James 1:19–20).

Love Is Calm And Slow to Anger

Loving leaders are not irritated by every little disagreement or frustration. The reason for this is that love, as we have already seen, is *patient*. Love suffers long with the wrongs inflicted by others. Those who control their anger control potentially explosive situations and bring healing to damaged emotions: "He who is slow to anger quiets contention" (Prov. 15:18).

Martyn Lloyd-Jones tells how Hudson Taylor was slow to anger and irritation. In China, standing at the bank of a large river, Hudson Taylor called for a riverboat to take him across the river. As the boat arrived at shore, a wealthy Chinese man came up behind Taylor in a hurry to get into the boat. The man pushed Hudson Taylor aside with such force that he fell into the mud. Horrified by what he had seen, the boatman refused to allow the wealthy man to board his boat because Taylor had been first to call for his services and was a foreigner who deserved, by Chinese customs, to be treated with respect. The rich man didn't realize Hudson Taylor was a foreigner because of his Chinese dress. When he realized what he had done, he instantly apologized. Hudson Taylor didn't react with irritation or anger; instead, he graciously invited the man to join him in the boat and witnessed to him of Christ's love.[12] He responded to a provoking situation according to the "more excellent way."

Chapter 6

Not Resentful or Joyful over Evil

*Love ... is not ... resentful; it does not rejoice at wrongdoing,
but rejoices with the truth.*
1 Corinthians 13:4–6

Despite R. C. Chapman's loving character, there were people who despised him. A local grocer in the city of Barnstaple, for example, was so upset at Chapman's open-air preaching that once he spit on him! For a number of years, the grocer continued to criticize and publicly interrupt Chapman's open-air preaching. Chapman continued on in his ministry and, when the opportunity presented itself, reached out to bless the grocer.

The opportunity came when one of Mr. Chapman's wealthy relatives came to visit him. The visit was more than just a social call. The relative wanted to see Chapman's ministry of hospitality and outreach to the city's poor. After an informative visit, the relative asked if he could buy groceries for the ministry. Mr. Chapman gladly agreed, but he insisted that the groceries be purchased at a certain grocer's shop—the one who had for so long vehemently maligned him.

Unaware of previous interactions between the grocer and Chapman, the relative went where he had been directed. He selected and paid for a large amount of food, then told the grocer to deliver it to Robert Chapman. The stunned grocer told the visitor that he must have come to the wrong shop, but the visitor explained that Chapman had sent him specifically to that shop. Soon the grocer arrived at Mr. Chapman's house, where he broke down in tears and asked for forgiveness. That very day, the grocer yielded his life to Christ!

"To forgive without upbraiding, even by manner or look," wrote Robert Chapman, "is a high exercise of grace—it is imitation of Christ."[1]

Love Does Not Hold Grudges or Seek Revenge

Another lofty, redeeming quality of love is that it is not resentful. The literal translation is love "does not reckon the evil." Commentator David Garland explains the imagery conveyed by these words: "Love does not keep books on evil.... The image is of keeping records of wrongs with a view to paying back injury."[2] Love does not hold grudges or seek revenge. It does not keep "a private file of personal grievances that can be consulted and nursed whenever there is possibility of some new slight."[3]

Jay Adams, a Christian counselor and author of numerous books on counseling, relates the story of a troubled couple who visited a Christian counselor for help. The wife's physician had advised her to see a counselor because she was developing an ulcer that apparently had no physical cause. During the session, the wife slammed down on the counselor's desk a manuscript "one-inch thick, on 8½ by 11 paper, typewritten on both sides ... a thirteen-year record of wrongs that her husband had done to her."[4]

If we enjoy nursing old wounds, we will be devoured by bitterness.

The counselor could immediately see that the wife's resentment of her husband's many faults and her meticulous documentation of each one had made her bitter. Keeping a record of her husband's sins had only made matters worse, to the point of causing this woman to become physically ill. So the counselor wisely reminded her of 1 Corinthians 13, emphasizing this: Love does not keep records of all the wrongs one has suffered at the hands of others.

The freedom not to keep records of wrongs suffered is vital to love. We all have been hurt by evil inflicted on us by others. We all have had to struggle with forgiveness. We all have had to let go of bad memories and give up any desire for revenge in order to be reconciled with those who have injured us. There is no way we could live happily together in marriage or with other believers in the local church without this quality of love. If we refuse to let go of emotional hurts, if we enjoy nursing old wounds, if we feel compelled to get even with our enemies, we will be devoured by bitterness, anger, and unforgiveness. We will be miserable examples and ineffective leaders for Christ.

Love Forgives

All the outstanding men and women of God through the ages have suffered terrible injustice and criticism, yet they have taken the opportunity to become forgiving people rather than resentful people. There is never an excuse for returning evil for evil or for destroying another person's life (Rom. 12:21). Being hurt is actually an opportunity to practice the "new commandment," to walk the royal road of love, to feed and care for your enemy, to "heap burning coals on his head," to "overcome evil with good" (Rom. 12:14, 19–21). It is an opportunity to suffer for the Lord's sake and to imitate God's forgiving love: "[Forgive] one another, as God in Christ forgave you.... Be imitators of God, as beloved children. And walk in love, as Christ loved us and gave himself up for us" (Eph. 4:32–5:2).

What a mighty power is love that can overcome evil, cover painful memories, forgive, forgo revenge, and arrest resentment. Love, Lewis Smedes writes,

> does not have to clear up all misunderstandings. In its power, the details of the past become irrelevant.... Accounts may go unsettled; differences remain unsolved; ledgers stay unbalanced. Conflict between people's memories of how things happened are not cleared up; the past stays muddled.... Love prefers to tuck all the loose ends of past rights and wrongs in the bosom of forgiveness—and pushes us into a new start.... [Moving] toward a reconciled life is one of the hardest things any human being is ever asked to do. Love is the power to do that.[5]

To choose the path of love doesn't mean we don't feel the pain of emotional injustice or struggle with anger or bad memories. We do feel the pain. However, choosing the "more excellent way" means that we seek, by the power and with the help of the Holy Spirit within us, to honestly deal with our emotional wounds. We forgive others just as we have been forgiven many times over by Christ. We seek to understand the person who has caused us injury and acknowledge that we have done the same to others. We confess our own bad attitudes, self-pity, and unforgiving heart. We see things from God's perspective, and we refuse to carry on the fight. We pray, and we go to the other person seeking authentic restoration and healing.

Scripture provides many examples of the power of forgiving love. When David heard that King Saul, who had tried to kill him many times, had died in battle, he "mourned and wept and fasted until evening for Saul and for Jonathan his son" (2 Sam. 1:12). David didn't gloat over Saul's death, although most people in David's position would have danced for joy. At the cross Jesus prayed, "Father, forgive them, for they know not what they do" (Luke 23:34). And Stephen, the first Christian martyr, also prayed for forgiveness for his executioners: "Lord, do not hold this sin against them" (Acts 7:60).

Other believers continue to give us good examples of the power of forgiving love. After Jim Elliot and his four companions (Pete Fleming, Roger Youderian, Ed McCully, and Nate Saint) were killed by the Auca Indians in the Amazon jungle of eastern Ecuador, his wife Elisabeth and the four other wives thought not of revenge but of love and forgiveness. A reporter who witnessed their reaction to the news gave this account:

> The widows believed that their husbands' death was not the meaningless tragedy it appeared to many. No thoughts of revenge crossed their minds; on the contrary, they felt with an increased sense of urgency the need to bring their message of love and redemption to the Aucas.[6]

Elisabeth Elliot later wrote,

> It gives me a much more personal desire to reach them. The fact that Jesus Christ died for all makes me interested in the salvation of all, but the fact that Jim loved and died for the Aucas intensifies my love for them.[7]

Nearly three years after the deaths of the five young missionaries, Elisabeth Elliot and Rachel Saint moved into an Auca village, the first foreigners ever to live among this fierce people. These women became friends and gospel messengers to the very men who killed their husbands. Today, as a result of those first encounters and the work of later missionaries, the New Testament has been translated and a church established. It is a remarkable story of Christian love and forgiveness.

Clara Barton, founder of the American Red Cross and known as the "Angel of the Battlefield," was a remarkable woman of lionhearted courage and sterling character. Like any prominent person she had critics. When a friend of hers reminded Clara of the criticism someone had made of her work, Clara couldn't remember it. Surprised, her friend said, "You don't remember it?" Clara's response is classic: "No, I distinctly remember forgetting it." Love makes a point of forgetting wrongs suffered.

African-American evangelist and social reformer John Perkins relates how he and other friends had been beaten nearly to death and tortured in a Mississippi jail for trying to help black people gain social equality and economic independence. For hours on end he was brutally kicked and stomped on, hit with blackjacks and billy clubs until he was bleeding and unconscious. Inebriated police officers held an unloaded gun to his head and pulled the trigger to taunt him. One officer forced a fork down his throat. They gave full vent to their vile hatred. Two years later, John was convalescing from a stomach operation. He was still waiting for civil justice, but as he lay in bed, he reflected on the suffering he had experienced and what God would have him do. He wrote:

> I began to see with horror how hate could destroy me—destroy me more devastatingly and suddenly than any destruction I could bring on those who had wronged me. I could try and fight back, as many of my brothers had done. But if I did, how would I be different from the whites who hate?
>
> And where would hating get me? Anyone can hate. This whole business of hating and hating back ... it's what keeps the vicious circle of racism going.
>
> The Spirit of God worked on me as I lay in that bed. An image formed in my mind. The image of the cross—Christ on the cross. It blotted out everything else in my mind.
>
> This Jesus knew what I had suffered. He understood. And He cared. Because He had experienced it all Himself.
>
> ... And He prayed God to forgive them. "Father, forgive these people, for they don't know what they are doing."

His enemies hated. But Jesus forgave. I couldn't get away from that.

The Spirit of God kept working on me and in me until I could say with Jesus, "I forgive them, too." I promised him that I would "return good for evil," not evil for evil. And he gave me the love I knew I would need to fulfill his command to me of "love your enemy."

Because of Christ, God himself met me and healed my heart and mind with his love.

… The Spirit of God helped me to really believe what I had so often professed, that only in the love of Christ is there any hope for me, or for those I had once worked so hard for.[8]

Life lived according to the "more excellent way" doesn't keep a journal of injustices and emotional hurts. It makes no plans to get even. Instead, "love is generous in her forgetfulness."[9] Love forgives and blesses those who have caused offense.

Love Is Not Joyful Over Wrongdoing

The eighth and final negative statement provides a perfect conclusion: Love "does not rejoice at wrongdoing" (1 Cor. 13:6). Love, writes Leon Morris, "takes no joy in evil of any kind."[10] Love cannot find distorted pleasure in injustice or unrighteousness because all such behavior hurts people and dishonors God. Love has no sympathetic attitude toward anything unrighteous. People who practice the "more excellent way" of love "abhor what is evil; hold fast to what is good" (Rom. 12:9).

In a secular world that often calls "evil good and good evil" (Isa. 5:20), there is, unfortunately, much joy over and approval of unrighteousness (Rom. 1:32). But it is astonishing how deeply "religious" people can also take great pleasure in wrongdoing. Those who masterminded the attacks on the World Trade Center in New York City on September 11, 2001, that killed and terrified thousands of innocent people relished their mission of death. Throughout the world, some people danced openly in delight while others gloated secretly. In the name of God and religion, people can lie, kill, and wage war.

Some Bible-believing Christians can also be found rejoicing in unrighteousness. An evangelical pastor, for example, announced gleefully from the pulpit that a brother in Christ who had opposed his ministry had died suddenly. He declared the man's death to be God's judgment. A deaconess spoke triumphantly to her friends of her success in driving out four different pastors through her phone calls and letter-writing campaigns. An elder bragged of enjoying a good fight and of humiliating his pastor and crushing the pastor's plans for the church. A pastor gloated when he heard of the misfortunes of people who had left his church. These "malignant joys" greatly grieve the Holy Spirit of God (Eph. 4:30). These are certainly not the behaviors of those who walk according to the "more excellent way" of love.

> "What a man rejoices in is a fair test of his character."
>
> —W. Graham Scroggie

Scroggie is very perceptive when he says, "What a man rejoices in is a fair test of his character. To be glad when evil prevails, or to rejoice in the misfortunes of others is indicative of great moral degradation."[11]

Loving people do not take pleasure in feelings of superiority over others. They do not delight in juicy gossip nor do they find satisfaction in hearing about the sordid sins and demise of Christian leaders they don't like. They do not gloat over scandals in a denomination to which they once belonged nor do they take pleasure in the fact that people who left their church have met with misfortune. They cannot feel glad when an earthquake in a nation they despise results in thousands of deaths. They don't enjoy publicly denouncing or criticizing the failures and errors of other Christians. And if they must expose and confront sinful behavior, they do it with compassion and genuine sadness of heart.

Loving leaders walk in the example of Job and David. Job was a loving community elder who could honestly say to his detractors, "[I have not] rejoiced at the ruin of him who hated me, or exulted when evil overtook him" (Job 31:29). David found no joy in defeating his nemesis. He refused to rejoice over opportunities to kill Saul, his mortal enemy (1 Sam. 24:1–7). On more than one occasion when David could easily have killed the king, he spared his life. Even Saul was forced to admit to David, "You are more righteous than I, for you have repaid me good, whereas I have repaid you evil" (1 Sam. 24:17). Saul never did understand David's remarkable love for him and his family. Petty, jealous leaders do not give people the benefit of the doubt, and they are not in the habit of thinking the best about others.

Love Rejoices with the Truth

To the last negative statement, love "does not rejoice at wrongdoing," Paul adds a positive counterpart: Love "rejoices with the truth." A loving heart is saddened by wrongdoing because it destroys people and displeases God. But the truth has just the opposite effect—it makes love sing for joy like a morning bird on a summer day. Love quickly recognizes conduct and attitudes that accord with the truth and takes great pleasure when truth prevails.

In this context, the word *truth* is used in the sense of righteous behavior or principles of conduct that correspond to the truth of the gospel message. Paul speaks not of "truth" in the abstract, but truth in practice that results in righteous living. Truth and righteousness are welded together in Christian faith. Love applauds all virtue and goodness, whether the person is a believer or an unbeliever. It rejoices in holy character, righteous conduct, integrity, and growth in Christ. "The person full of Christian love joins in rejoicing on the side of behavior that reflects the gospel—for every victory gained, every forgiveness offered, every act of kindness."[12]

Leaders and teachers who love people will tell you that one of their greatest delights is seeing those they lead grow in the faith and live obedient lives for Christ. I remember once sitting with a group of Christian college professors and teachers in a cafeteria and listening to them talk. They rejoiced over the progress of their students' lives as if they were talking about their team winning a world soccer match. To watch their students live according to the truth was their joy.

The father of the prodigal son rejoiced with great joy over his son's righteous repentance and return home (Luke 15:11–32). Luke records,

> while he was still a long way off, his father saw him ... and ran and embraced him and kissed him.... The father said to his servant, "Bring quickly the best robe, and put it on him, and put a ring on his hand, and shoes on his feet. And bring the fattened calf and kill it, and let us eat and celebrate." (Luke 15:20–23)

The prodigal's older brother, however, had no joy over his brother's repentance and homecoming because he did not have the love of God in his heart. Full of self-righteousness, "he was angry and refused to go in" to the celebration of his brother's homecoming. He would have rejoiced only at hearing of evil coming upon his brother or even of his death.

The tender heart of Paul rejoiced in all that the Corinthians did that was right and good, despite their many failures (1 Cor. 1:4–8; 11:2). He didn't inwardly gloat over God's discipline of some of the Corinthians for disobeying his instructions (1 Cor. 11:30). Their sufferings brought him no satisfaction or self-vindication. He could rejoice only at repentance, reconciliation, healing, godly conduct, and victory over the devil. To see his converts grow in love and walk in holy behavior delighted his heart.

John rejoiced over a brother named Gaius for living the Christian life according to the truth:

> For I rejoiced greatly when the brothers came and testified to your truth, as indeed you are walking in the truth. I have no greater joy than to hear that my children are walking in the truth. Beloved, it is a faithful thing you do in all your efforts for these brothers, strangers as they are, who testified to your love before the church. (3 John 3–6; also 2 John 4)

The proof that Gaius walked in the truth was the loving hospitality he showed to traveling Christians, most of whom were itinerant evangelists and teachers (3 John 5–8). It gave John great joy to hear that Gaius was kind, generous, and selfless.

Rejoicing in the truth, not wrongdoing, is living according to the "more excellent way" of love.

Chapter 7

Bears, Believes, Hopes, and Endures All Things

Love bears all things, believes all things, hopes all things, endures all things.
1 Corinthians 13:7

Love is tenacious. I once read a story of a criminally minded young man who continually got in trouble with the police for drugs and stealing. He was arrested and jailed several times and eventually was sent to prison for much of his remaining life. After a short time in prison, he was forgotten by his friends and even by his father. Outside the walls of his prison cell, he was a forgotten human being except for one person. Every week his mother would board a bus and travel several hours to visit him in prison. After a few hours of visitation, she would board the bus and return home. Almost daily she wrote letters and often sent books and personal items as allowed by prison officials. Neither distance, prison walls, money, or time could stop her from loving and visiting her son.

Some people think that loving people are weak and spineless. But nothing could be further from the truth. Unloving people are the ones who are weak because they are controlled by their petty, self-centered cravings. Jesus was the most loving person who ever existed, and he was not weak. He gave his life to save others. Paul's continual pursuit of the Corinthians after all the heartache they had caused him demonstrated not weakness but rather great strength and endurance.

Paul concludes and summarizes his description of love with four short, positive clauses that tell us what love does.[1] Love bears all things, believes all things, hopes all things, endures all things.

Love Bears All Things

Love bears up[2] under the heavy load of life's problems and sufferings. It holds steadfast and remains strong despite opposition, deprivation, and hard work.

Loving leaders persevere and do not give up easily or fall apart under pressure.

Love is courageous. It can carry enormous weight; thus loving leaders have an amazing ability to endure all sorts of suffering and frustration for the sake of others and the gospel (1 Cor. 9:12). This is a trait of all good shepherds (Gen. 31:38–40). They persevere and do not give up easily or fall apart under pressure.

Love Believes All Things

Paul next brings out faith and hope because of their connection with bearing and enduring all things. Faith and hope are the components of love that enable it to endure hardship and to bear up under the heavy burdens of life. In dealing with loved ones, love is not suspicious or cynical, but open and favorably disposed toward them. It seeks to understand each person in the best light with an understanding of life's complexities. It believes people can change and improve. It sees their worth, potential, and future possibilities. "It studies motives, and makes all possible allowances,"[3] says Scroggie. It is not afraid of being proved wrong or being embarrassed by others.

This doesn't imply that love is credulous or blind, for that would be a spurious faith. It is understood, although not directly stated, that love does not believe lies. Jesus' dealings with the Twelve, with their weaknesses and their failures, demonstrate the Christlike love that believes and hopes all things.

Love also trusts God and his Word and this makes all the difference in how one views and responds to people and difficult problems. Faith views people and life through the lens of God's sovereign purposes for his people.

Faith rests assured that "all things work together for good" for those who love God (Rom. 8:28). It believes nothing can "separate us from the love of God in Christ Jesus our Lord" (Rom. 8:39); "he who began a good work in you will bring it to completion at the day of Jesus Christ" (Phil. 1:6), and nothing is impossible with God.

Love Hopes All Things

The other core ingredient of love is hope. The situation in the church at Corinth was a mess, but Paul never gives up hope. He doesn't despair. He doesn't walk away from them in frustration. He writes letters, he visits, he sends representatives, and he prays. Despite his stern words, he has confidence that they eventually would respond properly.

Paul expresses his confidence in them: "I have great pride in you; I am filled with comfort. In all our affliction, I am overflowing with joy" (2 Cor. 7:4). "I rejoice, because I have complete confidence in you" (2 Cor. 7:16; see also 1:7; 2:3; 7:4, 14–16; 10:15).

This confidence is not a sentimental wish; it is faith in God's ultimate triumph and in God's good intentions for his people. This gives him realistic optimism and confidence in the future, even in the face of repeated difficulties and disappointments. Hope in the Lord and trust in his sure promises enable Paul to put problems and failures in perspective (Gal. 5:10; 2 Thess. 3:4; Philem. 21).

> Faith in God's ultimate triumph and in God's good intentions for his people gives realistic optimism even in the face of repeated difficulties and disappointments.

Love Endures All Things

This last quality, endurance, is similar to the first, "bears all things." Love is strong and tenacious: "No hardship or rebuff ever makes love cease to be love."[4] Love lasts; it holds out; it perseveres in the face of opposition, unkindness, and difficulties; it never gives up. Serving Christ and his people cannot be done without labor and self-sacrifice. Love gives a person the power to endure all things.

The life of Moses, Israel's greatest leader, illustrates that love bears up, believes, hopes, and endures all things. For forty trying years, he led the nation of Israel through the desert of Sinai. The people repeatedly complained about his leadership. They falsely accused him of abuse, ineptitude, evil motives, pride, and even trying to kill them and their children. At one time they were ready to stone him to death. Here are a few examples of their accusations and complaints:

- "Is it because there are no graves in Egypt that you have taken us away to die in the wilderness? What have you done to us in bringing us out of Egypt? ... Leave us alone that we may serve the Egyptians." (Ex. 14:11–12)
- And the whole congregation of the people of Israel grumbled against Moses and Aaron.... "You have brought us out into this wilderness to kill this whole assembly with hunger." (Ex. 16:2–3)
- The people quarreled with Moses.... So Moses cried to the Lord, "What shall I do with this people? They are almost ready to stone me." (Ex. 17:2–4)
- "Our wives and our little ones will become a prey. Would it not be better for us to go back to Egypt?" And they said to one another, "Let us choose a leader and go back to Egypt." (Num. 14:3–4)
- "Why have you made us come up out of Egypt to bring us to this evil place?" (Num. 20:5)

On one occasion his brother and sister spoke evil against him (Num. 12). They said, "Has the Lord indeed spoken only through Moses? Has he not spoken through us also?" (Num. 12:2). It must have been particularly painful for Moses when his own family and closest confidants attacked him. Yet he forgave them and prayed for their restoration after God judged them for their sinful accusations.

One of the worst moments of Moses' life was when 250 prominent leaders of the nation accused him of sinful, dominating leadership (Num. 16). They said to Moses and Aaron,

You have gone too far! ... Why then do you exalt yourselves above the assembly of the Lord? ... Is it a small thing that you have brought us up out of a land ... to kill us in the wilderness, that you must also make yourself a prince over us? Moreover, you have not brought us into a land flowing with milk and honey. (Num. 16:3, 13–14)

The people outright rejected Moses' authority and appointed a new leader to guide them back to Egypt (Neh. 9:17). On this occasion, Moses prayed to God to punish them for their wickedness, and God did. Their punishment was just and long overdue.

At other times, however, Moses prayed that God would not destroy the people. On four different occasions God was about to destroy the whole nation because of their continual rebellion, but Moses prayed and pleaded with God to spare them.[5] Moses probably could have thought of a hundred reasons not to pray for them, but as a man of God he was able to rise above personal feelings and pray for their forgiveness and deliverance.

Only love for God and love for the people could explain Moses' forbearance with the children of Israel. Love suffers long, love endures all things, love believes all things, and love hopes all things. Time after time, when it appeared that all was lost for the nation, Moses trusted, hoped, and endured. Selfish leaders, on the other hand, melt like snowflakes when the heat is on. They do not persevere.

Most significant ministry with people is usually long-term, but long-term ministry succeeds only with supernatural power from above to endure all of life's hardships and heartaches. Some missionaries serve for decades in dangerous areas where the problems and setbacks never end. How do they last? The answer: love for God and love for people. Love generates the faith, hope, and endurance to persevere through a lifetime of problems.

Chapter 8

The Greatest Thing
in the World

Love's power to endure (1 Cor. 13:7) leads to the final section of chapter 13 (vv. 9–13), where Paul makes two of his most profound declarations about Christian love: "Love never ends" and "faith, hope, and love abide, these three; but the greatest of these is love."

Love Is Eternal
1 Corinthians 13:8–12

In verse 8, Paul writes, "Love never ends." Technically this is not part of the fifteen descriptions of love in verses 4 through 7. Verse 8 begins a new section that contrasts the temporary nature of spiritual gifts with the permanent nature of love. This brings Paul directly back to his concern over the misuse of spiritual gifts in the church at Corinth (1 Cor. 12:1–13:3).

To show again that love is the "more excellent way," Paul tells his readers that spiritual gifts, no matter how impressive and important they appear, will someday cease: "As for prophecies, they will pass away; as for tongues, they will cease; as for knowledge, it will pass away" (1 Cor. 13:8). There will come a day when spiritual gifts will no longer be needed and will cease.

We will not need spiritual gifts in heaven. They are for the present age only. Love, in contrast, will never come to an end. It is for now and eternity.

In the concluding chapter of *Charity and Its Fruits*, Jonathan Edwards describes heaven as "a world of holy love"[1] and "the paradise of love."[2] Heaven will be a home filled forever with love because God is there and "God is love" (1 John 4:8).

When Christians love one another as Jesus did, the local church family prefigures the glories of our future loving, heavenly existence. Sadly, the church at Corinth was not experiencing heavenly love. It was characterized by rivalries, lawsuits, immorality, abuse of Christian liberty, disorderly conduct, pride, and selfish independence—altogether an unacceptably poor representation of the heavenly realities of love and the fruit of the Spirit.

Love Is the Greatest Virtue
1 Corinthians 13:13

The chapter closes with the familiar words: "So now faith, hope, and love abide, these three; but the greatest of these is love" (1 Cor. 13:13). Not every Christian is gifted with prophecy, tongues, or knowledge, but every Christian must be characterized by faith, hope, and love. This triad of virtues is fundamental to living the Christian life and to the maturing of the local church (1 Thess. 1:2–3).

Yet even among the three cardinal virtues of faith, hope, and love, Paul can say, "the greatest of these is love." So whether we are talking about spiritual gifts or cardinal virtues, love is the greatest! This is why every Christian leader and teacher must actively and intentionally "pursue love" (1 Cor. 14:1).

Summary of the Character and Behavior of a Loving Leader

Applying Paul's fifteen descriptions of love, we who lead and teach God's people are to be marked first by patience and kindness, even when we are wronged by those we serve. Our entire ministry is to be characterized by patience and kindness.

We are not to be self-centered leaders who are envious of those who are more talented or more popular than we are. Nor are we to put others down or boast about our own achievements. Most important, we are never to be arrogant and think of ourselves as superior to other people. We are to be humble and modest. We are not to be rude or ill-mannered but always tactful and conscious of proper social decorum. We are especially not to be self-seekers who look out first and foremost for our own interests and advantage. We are to be servants who build others up. We are not to be easily provoked to anger or irritability, which can be emotionally damaging to those we lead. We are to be calm, slow to anger, and never vindictive. We must not hold grudges but rather forgive and be gracious. Finally, we are not to rejoice in wrongdoing of any kind, but we are to rejoice with the truth.

We must always remember that love bears all things, believes all things, hopes all things, and endures all things.

A Plea for Self-Examination

I close this book with an important personal plea: Do not use this book to tell other people they have no love. Some of the most loving people I have ever known have been wrongfully accused of a lack of love.

In the Old Testament, the children of Israel accused Moses of unloving domination of the people, although he had saved their lives on many occasions and poured himself out to lead them for forty years. The truth is, the children of Israel were the unloving ones.

Most often, people who say that others have no love are themselves the ones most lacking. They think the new commandment says, "Love me or I'll destroy you and your church." They sit around waiting for other people to love them.

How easy it is to see the speck of lovelessness in another's eye but miss the log of self-centeredness, hypocrisy, and anger in your own eye (Matt. 7:3–5). *Use this book, therefore, to speak to yourself.* Strive to be an example to others of love according to the "more excellent way." And when a situation arises that demands confronting loveless behavior, you will have credibility as well as the skill to confront, "speaking the truth in love" (Eph. 4:15).

If we are honest, we must admit that we all have failed to love as we ought. So we should judge ourselves first. Only after we have confessed and repented of our own sins of lovelessness can we begin to help others to love. A good way to do that is to pray for them, because only God can change hearts.

Of course, even loving people do unloving things at times. They get into terrible conflicts and are not what they should be. Martin Luther, the sixteenth-century reformer, was a selfless, loving man, but he could also at times be cutting and harsh. The only perfectly loving person to grace this earth was the Lord Jesus Christ. The rest of us struggle all our lives to love as he loved and to figure out exactly how to love in difficult situations.

Endnotes

Notes to Chapter 1

1. William R. Moody, *The Life of Dwight L. Moody* (Chicago: Revell, 1900), 140. Also see Dwight Lyman Moody, *New Sermons, Addresses and Prayers* (Chicago: Goodspeed, 1877), 178.
2. Moody, *The Life of Dwight L. Moody*, 139.
3. Richard Ellsworth Day, *Bush Aglow: The Life Story of Dwight Lyman Moody, Commoner of Northfield* (Philadelphia: The Judson Press, 1936), 146; see also D. L. Moody, *Pleasure and Profit in Bible Study* (Chicago: The Bible Institute Colportage Association, 1895), 87.
4. Gregory J. Lockwood, *1 Corinthians*, Concordia Commentary (St. Louis: Concordia, 2000), 458.
5. John Short, "The First Epistle to the Corinthians," in *The Interpreter's Bible*, ed. Arthur C. Buttrick (New York: Abingdon-Cokesbury, 1953), 10:170.
6. George Sweeting, *Love Is the Greatest* (Chicago: Moody Press, 1974), 40.
7. George Müller was the founder and director of the Ashley Down Orphanage in Bristol, England; 122,683 orphans passed through this orphanage. Many biographies have been written on Müller's life of faith and prayer.
8. Rodney Stark, *The Rise of Christianity* (San Francisco: HarperCollins, 1996), 182.
9. *Martyrdom of S. Polycarp*, 18.
10. Jonathan Edwards, *Charity and Its Fruits* (1852; reprint ed., Edinburgh: Banner of Truth, 1978), 61–62.
11. D. A. Carson, *Showing the Spirit: A Theological Exposition of 1 Corinthians 12–14* (Grand Rapids: Baker, 1987), 60.
12. Sweeting, *Love Is the Greatest*, 117.
13. Jerry Bridges, *Growing Your Faith* (Colorado Springs: NavPress, 2004), 164–65.

Notes to Chapter 2

1. George Verwer, *The Revolution of Love* (Waynesboro, GA: OM Lit., 1993).
2. Ex. 34:6; Isa. 7:13; Jer. 15:15; Rom. 2:4; 9:22; Gal. 5:22; 1 Tim. 1:16; 2 Peter 3:9, 15.

3. Robert L. Peterson & Alexander Strauch, *Agape Leadership: Lessons in Spiritual Leadership from the Life of R. C. Chapman* (Colorado Springs: Lewis & Roth, 1991).

4. W. Graham Scroggie, *The Love Life: A Study of 1 Corinthians 13* (London: Pickering & Inglis, n.d.), 39.

5. Ruth 2:20; 2 Sam. 9:3; Ps. 106:7; 145:17; Luke 6:35; Rom. 2:4; 11:22; Eph. 2:7; Titus 3:4; 1 Peter 2:3.

6. William L. Lane, *The Gospel According to Mark,* NICNT (Grand Rapids: Eerdmans, 1974), 87.

7. Augustine, *Confessions,* trans. Henry Chadwick (Oxford: Oxford University Press, 1992), 88.

8. Alfred Tennyson, *Queen Mary* (Boston: James R. Osgood, 1875), 194.

Notes to Chapter 3

1. David E. Garland, *1 Corinthians*, BECNT (Grand Rapids: Baker, 2003), 8.

2. Nathaniel Vincent, *A Discourse Concerning Love* (1684; reprint ed., Morgan, PA: Soli Deo Gloria, 1998), 82.

3. W. Elfe Tayler, *Passages from the Diary and Letters of Henry Craik of Bristol* (London: Paternoster, n.d.), xiii.

4. His biographer notes:

> No feature of Mr. Craik's character was more conspicuous than that of love. It beamed forth in his countenance, it betrayed itself in the very tones of his voice, and his life was a practical comment on that word, "Do good to all." Hence his earnestness of manner in preaching; hence his acute sensibility in contemplating the prospects of humanity; hence his intense sympathy with the sorrows of others, and his extreme affection towards his friends, and especially the members of his family. Surely a more loving, sympathizing spirit has rarely left this world (Tayler, *Passages from the Diary and Letters of Henry Craik of Bristol,* 307).

5. Anthony C. Thiselton, *The First Epistle to the Corinthians*, NIGTC (Grand Rapids: Eerdmans, 2000), 1048.

6. John MacArthur, *1 Corinthians* (Chicago: Moody Press, 1984), 340.

7. W. Graham Scroggie, *The Love Life: A Study of 1 Corinthians 13* (London: Pickering & Inglis, n.d.), 40.

Notes to Chapter 4

1. The verb for "arrogant," *phusioō*, appears seven times in the New Testament, six of those in 1 Corinthians (4:6, 18–19; 5:2; 8:1; 13:4).

2. Quoted in Wayne A. Mack, *Humility: The Forgotten Virtue* (Phillipsburg, NJ: P&R Publishing, 2005), 61.

3. J. B. Phillips, *The New Testament in Modern English,* rev. ed., (New York: Macmillan, 1972), 361.

4. Jonathan Edwards, "Undetected Spiritual Pride," http://www.bibleteacher.org/ jedw_19.htm (accessed Sept. 19, 2005).

5. Lyle W. Dorsett, *Seeking the Secret Place: The Spiritual Formation of C. S. Lewis* (Grand Rapids: Brazos Press, 2004), 118.

6. Ibid, 41.

7. Ibid, 42.

8. C. S. Lewis, *Mere Christianity* (San Francisco: HarperCollins, 2001), 122.

9. Anthony C. Thiselton, *The First Epistle to the Corinthians*, NIGTC (Grand Rapids: Eerdmans, 2000), 1049.

10. See A. J. Broomhall, *Hudson Taylor & China's Open Century*, 7 vols. (London: Hodder and Stoughton).

11. Broomhall, *Hudson Taylor & China's Open Century*, vol. 5: *Refiner's Fire* (London: Hodder and Stoughton, 1985), 231.

Notes to Chapter 5

1. Lewis B. Smedes, *Love Within Limits: Realizing Selfless Love in a Selfish World* (Grand Rapids: Eerdmans, 1978), 42.

2. John Stott, *The Cross of Christ* (Downers Grove, IL: InterVarsity, 1986), 286.

3. Anthony C. Thiselton, *The First Epistle to the Corinthians*, NIGTC (Grand Rapids: Eerdmans, 2000), 1050.

4. Robert Law, *The Tests of Life: A Study of the First Epistle of St. John* (Edinburgh: T&T Clark, 1914), 72.

5. I. Howard Marshall, *The Epistles of John,* NICNT (Grand Rapids: Eerdmans, 1978), 126.

6. Timothy Dudley-Smith, *John Stott: A Global Ministry* (Leicester, England: InterVarsity, 2001), 21.

7. Ibid., 454.

8. Num. 16:15; Ps. 7:11; Nahum 1:2, 6; John 2:13–17; Eph. 4:26.

9. Jonathan Edwards, *Charity and Its Fruits* (1852; reprint ed., Edinburgh: Banner of Truth, 1978), 201.

10. Henry Drummond, *The Greatest Thing in the World* (1874, reprint ed., Burlington, ON: Inspirational Promotions, n.d.), 21–22.

11. Jonathan Edwards remarks, "Men are often [accustomed] to plead zeal for religion, and for duty, and for the honour of God, as the cause of their indignation, when it is only their own private interest that is concerned and affected. It is remarkable how forward men are to appear, as if they were zealous for God and righteousness, in cases wherein their honour, or will, or interest has been touched, and to make pretence of this in injuring others or complaining of them" (Edwards, *Charity and Its Fruits*, 198).

12. D. Martyn Lloyd-Jones, *Studies in the Sermon on the Mount*, 2 vols. (Grand Rapids: Eerdmans, 1971), 1:28–82.

Notes to Chapter 6

1. Robert L. Peterson and Alexander Strauch, *Agape Leadership: Lessons in Spiritual Leadership from the Life of R. C. Chapman* (Colorado Springs: Lewis & Roth, 1991), 39.

2. David E. Garland, *1 Corinthians*, BECNT (Grand Rapids: Baker, 2003), 618–19.

3. D. A. Carson, *Showing the Spirit: A Theological Exposition of 1 Corinthians 12–14* (Grand Rapids: Baker, 1987), 62.

4. Jay E. Adams, *Christian Living in the Home* (Grand Rapids: Baker, 1972), 33.

5. Lewis Smedes, *Love within Limits: Realizing Selfless Love in a Selfish World* (Grand Rapids: Eerdmans, 1978), 78–79.

6. Elisabeth Elliot, *The Savage My Kinsman* (Ann Arbor, MI: Servant Books, 1981), 6.

7. Ibid., 9.

8. John Perkins, *Let Justice Roll Down* (Glendale, CA: Regal Books, 1976), 204–06.

9. W. Graham Scroggie, *The Love Life: A Study of 1 Corinthians 13* (London: Pickering & Inglis, n.d.), 44.

10. Leon Morris, *The First Epistle of Paul to the Corinthians*, TNTC (Grand Rapids: Eerdmans, 1958), 185.

11. Scroggie, *The Love Life*, 45.

12. Gordon D. Fee, *The First Epistle to the Corinthians*, NICNT (Grand Rapids: Eerdmans, 1987), 639.

Notes to Chapter 7

1. Each of the four verbs has as its object the Greek word *panta*, "all things." However, the accusative case here "stands almost in the sense of an adverb": "always" or "in everything" (BDAG, s.v. *pas*, 783). The NIV and a number of commentators prefer this adverbial rendering. This avoids the idea that love gullibly believes "all things" and hopes "all things." It is difficult to be certain of the translation.

2. The Greek verb *stegō* can mean either (1) "covers," as in covering another's faults (NIV: "protects") or (2) "bears up under difficulty." Either meaning is possible here; however, the latter follows Paul's usage (1 Cor. 9:12; 1 Thess. 3:1, 5) and is favored.

3. W. Graham Scroggie, *The Love Life: A Study of 1 Corinthians 13* (London: Pickering & Inglis, n.d.), 46.

4. C. K. Barrett, *A Commentary on the First Epistle to the Corinthians*, HNTC (New York: Harper & Row, 1968), 305.

5. Ex. 32:10–14; Num. 14:12–20; 16:20–22, 41–50.

Notes to Chapter 8

1. Jonathan Edwards, *Charity and Its Fruits* (1852; reprint ed., Edinburgh: Banner of Truth, 1978), 325.

2. Ibid., 351.

Index of Authors

Additional Resources

These resources from Alexander Strauch will help you and your church nuture the love described in 1 Corinthians 13. They are available through your favorite bookseller or through the publisher.

LewisandRoth.com

800.477.3239 (USA)
719.494.1800 (International)

A Christian Leader's Guide to Leading with Love

Based on careful exposition of Scripture, Strauch presents the New Testament passages on love and applies them to leading people according to the "more excellent way" (1 Cor. 12:31). Whatever your leadership role is, you will be convicted, challenged and inspired to lead in the way of Christlike love.

A study guide is also available, making this a valuable tool for group study.

"This message is urgently needed by all of us. You may have talents and spiritual gifts, but without the love that his book talks about, you don't really have much at all." — George Verwer, Founder, Operation Mobilization

Love or Die: Christ's Wake-up Call to the Church

In his challenging exposition of Revelation 2:2–6, Strauch examines this alarming rebuke of Jesus Christ to his church. *Love or Die* reminds us that love can grow cold while outward religious performance appears acceptable—even praiseworthy.

A five-lesson study guide is included in the book.

"I can think of few books I've read recently that have had so immediate an impact on me and have given me so much to think about. I trust, that with God's help, the implications of this book will be with me always." — Tim Challies, challies.com.

If You Bite & Devour One Another: Biblical Principles for Handling Conflict

Conflict in churches is a pervasive problem we know all too well. In *If You Bite & Devour One Another*, Strauch examines the biblical passages on conflict and discusses key scriptural principles for handling various kinds of conflicts among Christians. The book emphasizes Spirit-controlled attitudes and behaviors through solid exposition and true-to-life stories of Christians handling conflicts in a Christ-honoring way.

A free study guide is also available for download at www.lewisandroth.com/free-downloads/.

"This book is urgently needed in the body of Christ.... I have put *Bite & Devour* into the top ten books that we are getting out across the world. It's a must read." — George Verwer, Founder, Operation Mobilization

Agape Leadership: Lessons in Spiritual Leadership from the Life of R. C. Chapman

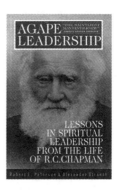

Agape Leadership promises to be one of the most spiritually inspiring books you've read. R. C. Chapman (1803–1902) provides an extraordinary example of Christlike, loving leadership. Charles Spurgeon, who knew Chapman, referred to him as "the saintliest man I ever knew."

Chapman became legendary in his own time for his gracious ways, his patience, his ability to reconcile people in conflict, his absolute fidelity to Scripture, and his loving pastoral care. By the end of his life, Chapman was known worldwide for his love, wisdom and compassion. In *Agape Leadership*, you will see godly, pastoral leadership in action through biographical snapshots from Chapman's life.

"This book ... should be read by everyone who calls on Christ as Lord. In so doing, you will be challenged to arrange your life in such a way that you are finding Christ to be your greatest and first love." — Terry Delaney, Christian Book Notes